Riot. Strike. Riot

Riot. Strike. Riot

The New Era of Uprisings

JOSHUA CLOVER

VERSO
London • New York

1 3 5 7 9 10 8 6 4 2

Verso
UK: 6 Meard Street, London W1F 0EG
US: 20 Jay Street, Suite 1010, Brooklyn, NY 11201
versobooks.com

Verso is the imprint of New Left Books

ISBN-13: 978-1-78478-059-3
eISBN-13: 978-1-78478-060-9 (US)
eISBN-13: 978-1-78478-061-6 (UK)

British Library Cataloguing in Publication Data
A catalogue record for this book is available from the British Library

Library of Congress Cataloging-in-Publication Data
A catalog record for this book is available from the Library of Congress

Typeset in Sabon by MJ & N Gavan, Truro, Cornwall
Printed in the US by Maple Press

for Oakland, for the commune

A. A violent order is disorder; and
B. A great disorder is an order. These
Two things are one. (Pages of illustrations.)
  —"The Connoisseur of Chaos," Wallace Stevens

You know how to get it, no money down, no money never,
money don't grow on trees no way, only whitey's got it,
makes it with a machine, to control you you cant steal
nothin from a white man, he's already stole it he owes you
anything you want, even his life. All the stores will open
if you will say the magic words. The magic words are: Up
against the wall mother fucker this is a stick up! Or: Smash
the window at night (these are magic actions) smash the
windows daytime, anytime, together, lets smash the window
drag the shit from in there. No money down. No time to
pay. Just take what you want.
  —"Black People!," Amiri Baraka

Contents

Acknowledgements

Like many other books of political theory, this book comes out of political mobilizations that in turn oriented reading groups, research, and countless discussions. In all those varied circumstances I have been grateful for the friendship, insight, and back-watching—literal and figurative—of Ian Balfour, Ali Bektaş, Lauren Berlant, Sean Bonney, Bruno Bosteels, Shane Boyle, Sarah Brouillette, Lainie Cassel, Maya Gonzalez, Virginia Jackson, Neil Larsen, Laura Martin, Phil Neel, Sianne Ngai, Will O'Connor, Simone Pinet, Nina Power, Louis-Georges Schwartz, Tim Simons, Michael Szalay, Alberto Toscano, Wendy Trevino, and Derek Zika. Probably forgot some. The initial formulations were invited by Beverly Silver, encouraged by William Sewell, and developed further in visits to Robert Brenner's Center for Social Theory and Comparative History and to the Arrighi Center for Global Studies. Making a book of it would not have been possible without the support of Sebastian Budgen and the folks at Verso, David Theo Goldberg and the University of California Humanities Research Institute, the University of Warwick Institute for Advanced Study, and the editorial assistance of Deborah Young.

Seeta Chaganti and Carol Clover have provided the conditions of possibility. I am particularly indebted to comrades whose thoughts and deeds are this book's nerves and sinews, including Aaron Benanav, Jasper Bernes, Chris Chen, Tim Kreiner, Colleen Lye, Annie McClanahan, Chris Nealon, and Juliana Spahr. *And when everything is at an end give me your hand so that we may begin again from the beginning.*

A Theory of Riot

Riots are coming, they are already here, more are on the way, no one doubts it. They deserve an adequate theory. A theory of riot is a theory of crisis. This is true at a vernacular and local level, in moments of shattered glass and fire, wherein riot is taken to be the irruption of a desperate situation, immiseration at its limit, the crisis of a given community or city, of a few hours or days. However, riot can only be grasped as having an internal and structural significance, to paraphrase Frantz Fanon, insofar as we can discover the historical motion that provides its form and substance. We must then move to further levels, where the gathering instances of riot are inextricable from ongoing and systemic capitalist crisis. Moreover, the riot as a particular form of struggle illuminates the character of crisis, makes it newly thinkable, and provides a prospect from which to view its unfolding.

The first relation between riot and crisis is that of surplus. This seems already a paradox, as both crisis and riot are commonly understood to arise from dearth, shortfall, deprivation. At the same time, riot is itself the experience of surplus. Surplus danger, surplus information, surplus military gear. Surplus emotion. Indeed, riots were once known as "emotions," a history still visible in the French word: *émeute*. The crucial surplus in the moment of riot is simply that of participants, of population. The moment when the partisans of riot exceed the police capacity for management, when the cops make their first retreat, is the moment when the riot becomes fully itself, slides loose from the grim continuity of daily life. The ceaseless social regulation that had seemed ideological and ambient and abstract is in this moment of surplus disclosed as a practical matter, open to social contest.

All these surpluses correspond to larger social transformations from which these experiences of affective and practical surplus are inextricable. These transformations are the material restructurings that respond to and constitute capitalist crisis, and which feature surpluses of both capital and population as core features. And it is these that propose riot as a necessary form of struggle.

"Any population has a limited repertoire of collective action," notes Charles Tilly, great historian of these matters. Writing in 1983, he takes the measure of a singular historical transformation, an oceanic shift whose tides spread late and soon across the industrializing world:

> Some time in the nineteenth century, the people of most western countries shed the collective-action repertoire they had been using for two centuries or so, and adopted the repertoire they still use today.[1]

The shift in question was that from riot to strike. Since the passage marked by Tilly, both tactics have existed within the repertoire; the question concerns which predominates, providing the primary orientation in the ceaseless war for survival and emancipation. The sense of the riot's receding character within this telling has been a commonplace. The

---

1 Charles Tilly, "Speaking Your Mind Without Elections, Surveys, or Social Movements," *The Public Opinion Quarterly* 47: 4, Winter 1983, 464.

opening sentence of the authoritative 1996 volume *Rioting in America* informs us, "Rioting is part of the American past."² But the past is never dead. It's not even past. In truth, another transformation was already in flight: since the sixties or seventies, the great historical shift has reversed itself. As the overdeveloped nations have entered into sustained, if uneven, crisis, the riot has returned as the leading tactic in the repertoire of collective action. This is true both in the popular imaginary and the realm of data (insofar as such matters give of statistical comparison). Regardless of perspective, riots have achieved an intransigent social centrality. Labor struggles have in the main been diminished to ragged defensive actions, while the riot features increasingly as the central figure of political antagonism, a specter leaping from insurrectionary debates to anxious governmental studies to glossy magazine covers. The names have become ordinal points of our time. The new era of riots has roots in Watts, Newark, Detroit; it passes through Tiananmen Square in 1989 and Los Angeles in 1992, arriving in the global present of São Paulo, Gezi Park, San Lázaro. The protorevolutionary riot of Tahrir Square, the nearly permanent riot of Exarcheia, the reactionary turn of Euromaidan. In the twilit core: Clichy-sous-Bois, Tottenham, Oakland, Ferguson, Baltimore. Too many to count.

Theory is immanent in struggle; often enough it must hurry to catch up to a reality that lurches ahead. A theory of the present will arise from its lived confrontations, rather than arriving on the scene laden with backdated homilies and prescriptions regarding how the war against state and capital ought be waged, programs we are told once worked and might now be refurbished and imposed once again

---

2 Paul A. Gilje, *Rioting in America*, Bloomington: Indiana University Press, 1999, 1.

on our quite distinct moment. The subjunctive is a lovely mood, but it is not the mood of historical materialism. Here we reach a sort of crossroad. Put in the most schematic terms, the association of Marx's analytic framework with a Leninist account of political strategy—one centered around proletarian organization toward the revolutionary party and the seizure both of state and production—is profoundly sedimented. The riot has no place in this conceptual landscape. Often enough riot is understood to have no politics at all, a spasmodic irruption to be read symptomatically and perhaps granted a paternalistic dollop of sympathy. Those who have accorded the riot the potential for an insurrectionary opening onto a social rupture come generally from intellectual and political traditions indifferent or even antithetical to the command of state and economy, most famously (but not exclusively) those of some strands of anarchism.[3]

This expresses a subterranean linking of communism, by skeptics as much as adherents, with "organization" as such, and further with a left party of order, with a scientific sense of history's progress, with modernity through which we must pass in all its machined barbarity. Contrarily, the riot, as is broadly agreed even among its partisans, is a great disorder.

The opposition of strike and riot thus comes to stand, via veiled syllogism, for the opposition of Marxism *tout court* to other intellectual and political trajectories, generally those that are antidialectical if not directly anticommunist traditions. Most if not all sides have taken part in this apportioning. There has been no shortage of books left and

---

3 The Invisible Committee, *The Coming Insurrection*, Cambridge: Semiotext(e), 2009, and its follow-up *To Our Friends*, trans. Semiotext(e), Cambridge: Semiotext(e), 2015, are the most incisive versions.

right that inform us, in tonalities now melancholy, now celebratory, that the waning of the labor movement and of the revolutionary class-mass party sequence, or the alleged transcendence of any labor theory of value, means that we may finally leave Marx's analysis and his categories to the twentieth century, if not the nineteenth. You will be familiar with the narration. The home counties of capitalism no longer feature an industrial working class of rising power or magnitude such that it can stand as a fraction for the exploited classes in general, much less lay hands on the levers of production. Moreover, the original focus on the English factory worker, and the accounting of such labor as peculiarly productive of value and thus closer to the heart of capital, has inevitably figured the subject of politics as white and male. Given the globalization of capital, its leap into all corners of social existence, and the vital developments of anticolonial politics (to shorthand a series of crucial and complex interventions), a new revolutionary subject will be needed, and a new revolutionary unfolding.

This is surely caricature. For all that, such suggestions are in many regards instructive if not simply true. This poses not a refutation of historical materialism but a set of problems for it. The waning of the traditional labor movements in the west and the intensification of a more thoroughgoing dispossession augur the end neither of potentially revolutionary anticapitalist antagonism nor of historical materialism's analytical force. Moreover, we will still require the latter to grasp the former.

After all, historical materialism is a theory of transformation if it is anything at all. This is not to say that every turn on the historical stage ought be affirmed. But a Marxism that can understand the tendency of reality only as error is no Marxism at all. The meaning of the riot has changed dramatically. It will not be understood without naming the determinations and forces according to which it takes on its new role, and by which it is driven forward irresistibly into the future, even as it looks backward on the seventeenth and eighteenth centuries. This then is the most basic necessity: a *properly materialist theorization of the riot*. Riot for communists, let's say.

It is not clear that such a volume exists. Perhaps the closest approach is Alain Badiou's *The Rebirth of History: Times of Riots and Uprisings*. "I, too, am a Marxist— naively, completely and so naturally there is no need to reiterate it," he insists, reiterating it in multiple while noting that he is

> well aware of the problems that have been resolved, and which it is pointless to start reinvestigating; and of the problems that remain outstanding, and which require of us radical rectification and strenuous invention. Any living knowledge is made up of problems, which have been or must be constructed or reconstructed, not of repetitive descriptions.[4]

Having offered this promissory note, he does not thenceforth wrestle greatly with the problematics of capital, nor make much use of the categories bequeathed us by the critique of political economy. We are left with "the Idea" playing the role vacated by the party, providing a coordination of revolutionary spirit that proceeds at some distance from the dialectical developments of social forces.

Badiou orders his book as a taxonomy of riots organized around the Arab Spring. This is one among the overlapping generic approaches to such studies, dividing up riots according to political status, to occasion or proximate

4   Alain Badiou, *The Rebirth of History: Times of Riots and Uprisings*, trans. Gregory Elliot, New York: Verso, 2012, 8.

cause, to coherence of participants. Another is the sociological study of rioters and their immediate conditions, and its close cousin the (generally first-person) phenomenology. Then there are the case studies of famous riots, alongside less glamorous surveys and atlases. Whatever its lacunae, the library of riot is dark and deep; only a fraction can be touched upon herein. This book has other promises to keep. It draws as well on Marx's value theory and the theory of crisis from which it cannot be disentangled, accounts of how urban sectors hollow out, how entire sectors of the economy rise and fall, and how the capitalist world-system is ordered and disordered; the tradition of world-systems analysis provides a framework of both global breadth and *longue durée* within which to think the localized event of the riot.

There are limits to this extension, necessarily. It is evident that riots in India and China, to choose only two contemporary examples, have their own distinct characteristics (and their own developing scholarship). My claims mostly concern the early industrializing and now deindustrializing nations of the west. These places do not have a privileged claim on riots; they are, rather, the terrain in which a particular logic becomes visible, a logic of both riot and of capital in its catastrophic autumn. The claims are, I hope, somewhat portable for all that, embedded in political-economic changes that are themselves bound to travel.

Moreover, just as the new era of riots expresses capital's global transformations and thus bears capital's objective conditions, it becomes an occasion to peer more deeply into those transformations. If this book offers any novelties, they are these. First, clarified definitions of *riot* and *strike*, which suffer from more confusion than one might expect. Second, an explanation of why the riot has returned and why it takes the form it does in the present. And third, once a logic of riot and its relation to transformations of capital has been derived, some forecasts about the future of struggle. A theory of the present, then. At a minimum, the theory should be able to explain why, following the failure to return an indictment against the police officer who murdered Michael Brown in Ferguson, Missouri, there was a national wave of riots—and why, as if by a telepathy of the immiserated, the riots in city after city took the form of blocking the nearest available freeway.

Riot-Strike-Riot Prime

This book is arranged more or less chronologically, from the golden age of riot through the age of strikes and back again, with a particular focus on the transitional passages. However, it is not a chronicle. Rather, it takes the opportunity to develop a series of concepts and arguments about riot and political economy as it moves. It builds an explanatory model that can coordinate the basic facts of the present, such that they might testify a bit more eloquently. As it approaches the current era, the chapters inevitably get a bit more detailed. Nonetheless, the whole will necessarily be a simplification of reality's endless complexities; such are heuristic models. At least this makes for shorter books.

King George I's Riot Act in 1714, responding in part to the Coronation Riots attending his ascension, declares itself "An act for preventing tumults and riotous assemblies, and for the more speedy and effectual punishing the rioters." It raises a question about the riot's communicative status from the outset. It is in no small regard about declaration, about speech—it prescribes the language that must be read to declare an assembly unlawful (hence "reading the Riot Act"). With it, the term *riot* modulates decisively from its older sense of "Wanton, loose, or wasteful living; debauchery, dissipation, extravagance" and even "unrestrained revelry, mirth or noise" to its contemporary meaning of "a violent disturbance of the peace by an assembly or body of persons; an outbreak of active lawlessness or disorder among the populace." Chaucer's usage, as so often, presages the word's modernity. "For thefte and riot, they been convertible," he writes in "The Cook's Tale," noting that the master pays the price for the apprentice's revelry.[5] He associates the word with the overturning of social hierarchies.

Transition from riot to strike takes hold unevenly. The arrival of the strike as social fact falls somewhere between 1790 and 1842, the date of the first massive strike in England. Like many sea changes, it is as hard to recognize at first, as it will prove entirely apparent in later view. It will be useful to recognize the continuity as well as the opposition, the way that new content for struggle emerges from older forms of action and thus goes through periods of ambiguity. The same might be said of the later return to riot; it is early yet. With the waning of the labor movement in the west the riot ascends, both relatively and absolutely. Inevitably, there is an interval when the two tactics coexist alongside each other. From one perspective, they seem to vie for primacy; from another, the volatility of their dual presence during this second transition provisions a revolutionary situation, one known widely and not entirely accurately by the name "1968." The world-historical year of 1973 is the swivel, with the collapse of industrial profits signaling the onset of what should rightly be called the Long Crisis, with its recompositions of class and global division of labor that progressively undermine the possibilities for

---

5   "For thefte and riot, they been convertible." Geoffrey Chaucer, *The Riverside Chaucer*, 3rd ed., Larry D. Benson, gen. ed., Boston: Houghton Mifflin, 1987, 85.

militant labor organization in the west. By the eighties, the transition is largely complete. If this first appears as part of a more widespread closure of revolutionary frontiers—as the end of history concomitant with the exit of twentieth-century communisms—that verdict is once again open to debate. The debate is inextricably wound up with the riot's return.

Riot-strike-riot, then. But that won't quite do. Such a formulation can't help but suggest a simple oscillation, or worse, an atavistic reversion. That story has its appeals, given the affective tonalities of the present, the intimations of civilizational collapse accelerated by ecological catastrophe. Still, it's just a shape, not a theory. It is neither explanatory nor accurate. The new era of riots in many ways does not resemble its predecessor. Previous to the nineteenth century, general difficulties faced by the poor in managing subsistence, including not just bread riots but the common anti-enclosure riot—provided the occasion for social antagonism to burst forth. Notably, these events included "export riots," episodes in which the shipping of grain out of county, especially in times of famine, was halted by concerted and coordinated efforts. By many accounts, this basic configuration of needs obtains today; positivistic studies linking food prices to riots remain common, and in some ways persuasive, particularly in low-wage nations. Nonetheless, riot after riot begins now not at the granary but at the police station, literally or figuratively, incited by the police murder of a young person with dark skin, or following on the failure of the legal apparatus to hold the police adequately responsible for their violence. The new era finds its paradigm in the Los Angeles riots of 1992, following the acquittal of the officers who were recorded beating Rodney King brutally after a traffic stop—riots which spread to numerous other cities and continued for five days. Increasingly, the contemporary riot transpires within a logic of racialization and takes the state rather than the economy as its direct antagonist. The riot returns not only to a changed world but changed itself.

Riot-strike-riot prime. Better. These terms provide the book's three sections. Each has not just a proper period but a proper place. For the first era of riot, the market, but even more the port; for the era of strike, the factory floor; and, for the new era of riot, square and street. To make good on this tripartite sequence, this book will need to discover both the continuity of the two eras of riots as well as their difference: the unity of a tumult in the marketplace and the often racialized upwellings directed apparently against the state. Here then is the argument, in its condensed and abstracted form, to which the remainder of the book will add both particulars and digressions, as well as a political-economic framework and a glance forward.

The Marketplace and the Factory Floor

The primary difficulty in defining the riot devolves from its profound association with violence; for many, this association is so affectively charged in one direction or another that it is difficult to dispel and in turn difficult to notice other things. No doubt many riots involve violence —perhaps the great majority, if one includes property damage in the category, as well as threats explicit or *sub voce*. It is not altogether clear that such inclusion is natural or reasonable. That property damage equals violence is not a truth but the adoption of a particular set of ideas about property, one of relatively recent vintage, involving specific identifications of humans with abstract wealth of the sort that culminate in, for example, the legal holdings that corporations are people.

However, this insistence on the violence of the riot effectively obscures the daily, systematic, and ambient violence that stalks daily life for much of the world. The vision of a generally pacific sociality that only in exception breaks forth into violence is an imaginary accessible only to some. For others—most—social violence is the norm. The rhetoric of the violent riot becomes a device of exclusion, aimed not so much against "violence" but against specific social groups.

Moreover, across more than two centuries, strikes quite often involved violence as well: pitched battles between workers on one side and cops, scabs and mercenaries on the other, which at their zenith resembled military engagements. If one extends the category as above, violence is ubiquitous in the strike, even as a kind of defensive counterviolence. Reporting from France in 1968, the Italian poet Angelo Quattrochi noted,

> Workers can threaten to smash the machinery, and the threat alone can prevent an armed intervention. Masters of the factory, their condition of dispossession is their very strength. The machines, the Capital, owned by others and by others manipulated, are now in their hands.[6]

This passage intends to distinguish the limited strike, for Quattrochi a craven and choreographed event, from the factory occupation. It is suggestive that he chose to make the distinction in that moment, peering down at a Paris where riot and strike have entered into vivid collaboration and competition, each trying to transcend not just its

---

6 Angelo Quattrochi, "What Happened," in *The Beginning of the End: France, May 1968*, eds. Angelo Quattrochi and Tom Nairn, New York: Verso, 1998, 49.

own but the other's limits. That said, the limited strike's gray servility is itself a particular historical development. The real situation he describes, the potential for workers to dispose of the gears of production as they see fit is at the heart of the strike.

But this is already to have implied that we know the difference between riot and strike. If not violence, what then? E. P. Thompson, whose thought is this book's lodestone, provides the basis for an answer in his epochal "The Moral Economy of the English Crowd in the Eighteenth Century." If this answer has gone curiously overlooked, it is almost certainly because the essay never quite formalizes the logic it makes available. Taking issue with the reductions and depoliticizing force cached within the term "bread riot," he produces a more systematic vision of the riot's political economy:

> It has been suggested that the term "riot" is a blunt tool of analysis for so many particular grievances and occasions. It is also an imprecise term for describing popular actions. If we are looking for the characteristic form of direct action, we should take, not squabbles outside London bakeries, nor even the great affrays provoked by discontent with the large millers, but the "risings of the people" (most notably in 1740, 1756, 1766, 1795 and 1800) in which colliers, tinners, weavers and hosiery workers were prominent. What is remarkable about these "insurrections" is, first, their discipline, and, second, the fact that they exhibit a pattern of behaviour for whose origin we must look back several hundreds of years: which becomes more, rather than less, sophisticated in the eighteenth century; which repeats itself, seemingly spontaneously, in different parts of the country and after the passage of many quiet years. The central action in this pattern is not the sack of granaries

and the pilfering of grain or flour but the action of "setting the price."[7]

This is precisely the situation that will turn with the century:

> Economic class-conflict in nineteenth-century England found its characteristic expression in the matter of wages; in eighteenth-century England the working people were most quickly inflamed to action by rising prices.[8]

Thompson catches the texture of deep transformation in flight, elusive as it is immanent:

> We are coming to the end of one tradition, and the new tradition has scarcely emerged. In these years the alternative form of economic pressure—pressure upon wages—is becoming more vigorous; there is also something more than rhetoric behind the language of sedition—underground union organization, oaths, the shadowy "United Englishmen." In 1812 traditional food riots overlap with Luddism. In 1816 the East Anglian laborers do not only set the prices, they also demand a minimum wage and an end to Speenhamland relief. They look forward to the very different revolt of laborers in 1830. The older form of action lingers on into the 1840s and even later: it was especially deeply rooted in the Southwest. But in the new territories of the industrial revolution it passed by stages into other forms of action.[9]

---

7 E. P. Thompson, "The Moral Economy of the English Crowd in the Eighteenth Century," *Past and Present*, no. 50, Feb. 1971, 107–8.
8 Ibid., 79.
9 Ibid., 128–9.

Prices and wages, this is the pairing. One the measure of the marketplace, the other that of the factory floor and the mine, of agricultural labor once commonly held lands and subsistence farming have gone down amid blood and fire. R. H. Tawney makes much the same point, in somewhat different terms:

> The economy of the mediaeval borough was one in which consumption held somewhat the same primacy in the public mind, as the undisputed arbiter of economic effort, as the nineteenth century attached to profits.[10]

But wages are themselves a special kind of price. Reminding ourselves of this, the formula becomes clear: In the first instance, *riot is the setting of prices for market goods, while strike is the setting of prices for labor power.* This is the first level or horizon of analysis required for understanding the history of riot, which we might call the practical level. The political practice in its fullest dimension is that of reproduction—of the household and the individual, of the local community. Around the turn from eighteenth to nineteenth century, the matter of reproduction shifts its center of gravity from one location to another, one struggle to the next.

Consumer and worker are not two opposed, much less successive, classes, it should go without saying. Rather, they are two momentary roles within the collective activity required to reproduce a single class: the emergent modern proletariat, who must make their way within the wage-commodity nexus. If one moment takes precedence over the other, this speaks to the given degree of technical and social development within that nexus, and the position

10 R. H. Tawney, *Religion and the Rise of Capitalism*, London: Harcourt Brace, 1926, 33.

the proletarian holds in relation. In the scene of riot, those setting prices in the marketplace may be laborers (note Thompson's "colliers, tinners, weavers and hosiery workers") but this is not the immediate fact that has brought them there. This recognition allows a refinement of our definitions.

The strike is the form of collective action that

1) struggles to set the price of labor power (or the conditions of labor, which is much the same thing: the amount of misery that can be purchased by the pound);
2) features workers appearing *in their role as workers;*
3) unfolds in the context of capitalist production, featuring its interruption at the source via the downing of tools, cordoning of the factory floor, etc.

The riot is the form of collective action that

1) struggles to set the price of market goods (or their availability, which is much the same thing, for the question is similarly one of access);
2) features participants with no necessary kinship but their dispossession;
3) unfolds in the context of consumption, featuring the interruption of commercial circulation.

This apparatus is simple but powerful, and suffices for the span first surveyed by our scholars, well into the twentieth century. It nonetheless poses problems for the present. The characteristic struggles of *riot prime*, the period beginning in the sixties alongside the strike's last flourishing, and continuing into the present, cannot finally be understood adequately within the framework of price-setting, even in

Thompson's expanded sense. But neither can it be understood without it. It is here that we will require a second level or horizon: that of periodization, concerned precisely with the degree of capital's technical and social development referred to above, in all its eloquent and ambiguous undulations.

Circulation-Production-Circulation Prime

We have noticed already that the first transition, *riot-strike*, corresponds both historically and logically to the Industrial Revolution and its extension and intensification of the wage relation at the beginning of Britain's long nineteenth century. The second transition, *strike-riot prime*, corresponds in turn to the period of "hegemony unraveling" at the end of the United States' long twentieth century. A rise and a fall. A certain shapeliness amid the mess and noise of history delivering us now to the autumn of empire known variously by the terms *late capitalism, financialization, post-Fordism*, and so forth—that dilating litany racing to keep pace with our protean disaster.

These datings are drawn from the schema of Giovanni Arrighi, who describes four "long centuries and systemic cycles of accumulation."

"The main feature of the temporal profile of historical capitalism sketched here is the similar structure of all long centuries," notes Arrighi.[11] The recurrent structure is a tripartite sequence beginning with a financial expansion originally led by merchant capital; material expansion "of the entire world-economy" led by manufacturing or more broadly industrial capital, in which capital accumulates systemically; and when that has reached its limits, a final

---

11   Giovanni Arrighi, *The Long Twentieth Century: Money, Power, and the Origins of Our Times*, London: Verso, 1996, 219–20.

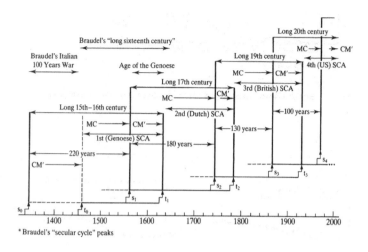

* Braudel's "secular cycle" peaks

financial expansion. During this phase, no real recovery of accumulation is possible, but only more and less desperate strategies of deferral. Historically, the financial sector of the leading economy has in such a situation found a rising industrial power to soak up its excess capital, thus bank-rolling its own replacement. This new hegemon will form on necessarily expanded grounds, able to restore accumu-lation on a global scale but by the same token beginning from a position closer to its own limits for expansion—thus Arrighi's overlapping cycles, broadening and quickening as they go, the series of transfers once known as *translatio imperii*.

This schematization has been occasion for various inquiries about the transition to capitalism often found under the heading "Commerce or Capitalism?" Robert Brenner, Ellen Meiksins Woods and others have argued that the development of extensive trading networks and accom-panying social reorganization should not be confused with capitalism proper, and particularly not with capital's "relentless and systematic development of the productive forces," which cannot be said to have started much before the British cycle and industrial takeoff.[12] It is precisely this distinction that animates the argument herein. Markets inarguably predate capitalism and continue within it; they become part of capitalism's constitution only once they are transformed by the elaboration of the wage-commodity nexus and subjected to the disciplines of surplus-value production. This tracks the first transition, *riot-strike*.

And yet it is hard to dispute Arrighi's finding that protocapitalist commercial empires followed much the same developmental parabola as their more realized versions. The two great capitalist empires of Britain and the United States preserve and transmute the developmental forms, filling them with new content. Within the spiraling reach of capital, each cycle features a phase dominated by the logic of production, here meaning the valorization of commodities, which Arrighi generalizes as M-C. Bracketing this are phases dominated by circulation, for such is the character of merchant or finance capital, which Arrighi defines as the realization of values, or C-M. It is never either/or. Both processes must be in conjoined flight or capital would cease to move altogether (and immobile capital is not capital at all). The description here concerns the balance of forces within the expanded circuit of capital.

We have therefore a periodization to match our practices: *riot-strike-riot prime* maps onto phases of *circulation-production-circulation*. True, the period bracketing the beginning of the twentieth century was for Britain, still at the time the leading capitalist economy, a financial or circulation-centered period. Here, the reasoning of Arrighi's overlap-based schema comes clear. While the United States experienced its own "Long Depression" corresponding to Britain's economic shift at the heel of the nineteenth

---

12 Robert Brenner, *The Economics of Global Turbulence*, London: Verso, 2009, 13.

century, it nonetheless oversaw in this period a notable expansion of production driven by a second Industrial Revolution able to counterbalance the British decline. Our current phase of circulation, however, lacks much evidence of such systemic counterbalance; for all the attention paid to China's role as the new workshop to the world, e.g., it is already shedding industrial labor.[13]

Indeed, this gestures toward what is unique, at least provisionally, about our moment within a world-systems frame. The spiraling reach of long centuries may have run out of room to expand; reformation on a larger scale does not seem to be in the cards (though we should not too easily dismiss capital's ability to rescue itself from seemingly total crisis). Productive capital held sway from, say, 1784 to 1973. It may yet again. For the moment, this seems uncertain. Far from underwriting a rising hegemon, the United States in its decline is—despite its hypertrophied financial sector—ending its run as a massive debtor nation. It is now possible to argue that, even at a global or systemic level, capital finds itself in a phase of circulation not being met by rising production elsewhere—a distinct phase we will inevitably have to name *circulation prime*.

Accordingly, the British and U.S. regimes can be melded into a single metacycle following the sequence *circulation-production-circulation prime*. Again, this requires a certain heuristic smoothing of the capitalist world-system's volatile trajectory. It is an argument, not a plain truth. Still, we think it is a suggestive one: it is possible to map Arrighi's three phases onto Brenner's periodization of capital in what can be seen as an "arc of accumulation," at least in the west, rising from commerce with the Industrial Revolution

13   Alan Freeman, "Investing in Civilisation: What the State Can Do in a Crisis" in *Bailouts and Bankruptcies*, eds., Julie Guard and Wayne Antony, eds., Winnipeg: Fernwood, 2009.

and descending into finance with widespread deindustrialization, with no reversal in view. The coeval sequence of *riot-strike-riot prime* becomes therefore a history of capitalism and an exposition of its current form, of the contradictions of the present.

Riot and Crisis

For the return of the riot to serve as testimony about the status of capitalism as such, there must be more than a coincidence between the two sequences. There must be a theoretical enchainment. This is the third and final level of analytical horizon, that of history itself, by which we mean the dialectical twining of lived struggles with the compulsions of capital's self-moving motion, understood as a real movement of social existence. What within the objective motion of capital joins riot to circulation, strike to production, and moves us from one to the next?

This question has already been given a preliminary answer. Phases led by material production will issue forth struggles within production, over the price of labor power; phases led by circulation will see struggles in the marketplace, over the price of goods. This is a synchronic account, lacking a dynamic that drives us from phase to phase; moreover, it does not yet address the peculiarities of *riot prime* and *circulation prime*. That requires a swift pass through the Marxian theory of crisis.[14]

Value, for Marx, has both a qualitative existence as a social relation and a quantitative existence in exchange

---

14 It is frequently noted that Marx did not leave behind a completed theory of crisis. His value theory in general, however, provides the logical basis for an elaborated theory. For the best summary of this, see Anwar Shaikh, "Introduction to the History of Crisis Theories," *US Capitalism in Crisis*, New York: URPE, 1978.

value.[15] The exchange value borne by a commodity allows for surplus value, the "invisible essence of capital," valorized in production and realized as profit in circulation. Circulation, Marx is at pains to decipher, can never itself be the source of new value for capital as a whole. The idea that it could receives an extended and scorn-laced treatment in *Capital* that ends:

> However much we twist and turn, the final conclusion remains the same. If equivalents are exchanged, no surplus value results, and if nonequivalents are exchanged, we still have no surplus-value. Circulation, or the exchange of commodities, creates no value.[16]

These categories are endlessly troubled, not least by the limits of "circulation." The extraordinary development of transport, one of the hallmarks of our time, would seem at first to fit the bill, circulating products toward realizing as profit the surplus value valorized elsewhere. The change of location, some argue contrarily, increases the value of a commodity. In its most restricted sense, "pure circulation costs" might be limited to activities that make nothing but exchange itself, the abstract transfer of title: sales, bookkeeping, and the like. Moreover, financialization and "globalization" (by which we mean the extension toward planetary limits of logistical networks and processes, coordinated by advances in information technologies) should also be understood as temporal and spatial strategies respectively to internalize new value inputs from elsewhere

---

15 For the most eloquent gloss of this portion of Marx's theory, see I. I. Rubin, *Essays on Marx's Theory of Value*, trans. Fredy Perlman and Milos Samardzija, New York: Black Rose, 1990, 120–21.

16 Karl Marx, *Capital: A Critique of Political Economy*, vol. 1, London: Penguin, 1992, 226.

and elsewhen. But this can only affirm the proposition that the current phase in our cycle of accumulation is defined by the collapse of value production at the core of the world-system; it is for this reason that capital's center of gravity shifts toward circulation, borne by the troika of Toyotaization, information technology, and finance.

Here, practical facts prove illuminating. As Brenner notes:

> Between 1973 and the present, economic performance in the US, western Europe, and Japan has, by every standard macroeconomic indicator, deteriorated, business cycle by business cycle, decade by decade (with the exception of the second half of the 1990s).[17]

Global GDP growth from the fifties through the seventies remained higher than 4 percent; since then, it has rested at 3 percent or lower, sometimes much lower.[18] Even the best of times during the Long Crisis have been by and large worse than the worst of times in the preceding long boom. Were we to stipulate that transport may be part of valorization as well as realization, we would nonetheless confront the fact that the great build-outs of global transport and the acceleration of turnover time since the seventies are concurrent with the retreat of industrial production in the leading capitalist nations. This lockstep march is in turn concomitant with exactly what value theory projects from a shift toward circulation: less value production, fewer systemic profits. By any measure, shipping and finance do not seem to have arrested the stagnation and decline in

---

17 Robert Brenner, "What's Good for Goldman Sachs," prologue to Spanish edition of *The Economics of Global Turbulence*, Madrid: Akal, 2009. Made available to the author in typescript, 6.

18 Ibid., 8.

global profitability. Borrowing a term from Gilles Chatelet, we might call their collaboration "cybermercantilism," cognate to the preindustrial mode in which no amount of buying cheap and selling dear or selling more and more can lead to expansion.

But this is not to say they have not bolstered the profits of individual firms, which can gain competitive advantage by decreasing their own circulation costs in a game of beggar-your-neighbor for the age of information technology. Similarly, firms can enter into schemes that recirculate and redistribute already extant value, skimming a portion as it passes. Without going too far into the Marxological maze, we can affirm rather uncontroversially about the period in question that capital, faced with greatly diminished returns in the traditionally productive sectors, goes looking for profit beyond the confines of the factory—in the FIRE sector (Finance, Insurance, and Real Estate), along the lanes laid out by global logistical networks—yet finds there no ongoing solution to the crisis that pushed it from production in the first place. Instead, ever more frenetic churning, more elaborate schemes, larger bubbles, bigger busts.

In a motion of dialectical despair, the very thing that has sent capital into the fratricidal zero-sum sphere of circulation does much the same for a rising portion of humanity. Crisis and unemployment, the two great themes of *Capital*, are both expressions of capital's tragic flaw: that, in seeking profit, it must destroy profit's wellspring, careering into objective limits in its unrelenting drive for accumulation and productivity. The *Grundrisse* offers the most concise formulation:

> Capital itself is the moving contradiction, [in] that it presses to reduce labor time to a minimum, while it posits

labor time, on the other side, as sole measure and source of wealth. Hence it diminishes labor time in the necessary form so as to increase it in the superfluous form; hence posits the superfluous in growing measure as a condition—question of life or death—for the necessary.[19]

The "moving contradiction" is nothing but the law of value itself in motion, presenting itself in various forms. One might see it as the contradiction between value and price, the measures of production and circulation respectively—which will turn out to be as well the contradiction between capital as a whole and individual capitals. The latter do not concern themselves with the overall health of the capitalist system, nor are they compelled to do so. They are compelled, rather, to outcompete other capitals in their sector. So, whereas the need to expand, to generate new value leading to systemic accumulation, is an existential absolute from the standpoint of all capital, individual capitalists do not think in terms of value and accumulation. They measure their existence in price and wealth, and are compelled to seek profit wherever it may be found, regardless of the consequences for the whole.

No less is this unitary phenomenon a contradiction between absolute and relative surplus value. Intercapitalist struggles to economize all processes iteratively replace labor power with more efficient machines and organizational forms, and so over time increase the ratio of constant to variable capital, dead to living labor, expelling the source of absolute surplus value in the struggle for its relative form.

Crisis is development of these contradictions to the breaking point. This features not a shortage of money but

---

19   Karl Marx, *Grundrisse*, London: Penguin Books, 1993, 706.

its surplus. Accrued profit lies fallow, unable to convert itself into capital, for there is no longer any seductive reason to invest in further production. The factories go quiet. Seeking wages elsewhere, displaced workers discover that labor-saving automation has generalized itself across the various lines. Now unused labor piles up cheek by jowl with unused capacity. This is the production of nonproduction.

Here, we have returned under somewhat different cover to the matter of class, in the form of what Marx calls "surplus population, whose misery is in inverse ratio to the amount of torture it has to undergo in the form of labor. The more extensive, finally, the pauperized sections of the working class, and the industrial reserve army, the greater is official pauperism. *This is the absolute general law of capitalist accumulation.*"[20] As *Endnotes* points out in the most incisive treatment of this issue: "This surplus population need not find itself completely 'outside' capitalist social relations. Capital may not need these workers, but they still need to work. They are thus forced to offer themselves up for the most abject forms of wage slavery in the form of petty production and services —identified with informal and often illegal markets of direct exchange arising alongside failures of capitalist production."[21]

It cannot be surprising that this surplus population is racialized across the west. Capital's capacity for profit has always required the production and reproduction of social difference; in slack labor markets, the apparatus of wage differentials makes the leap from quantitative to qualitative. Alongside the "jobless recoveries" since

---

20 Karl Marx, *Capital*, vol. 1, 798 (emphasis in original).
21 "Misery and Debt," *Endnotes* 2, 2010, 30, fn15.

1980 that lend support to underlying theories of growing surplus, the unemployment rate among, for example, black Americans has consistently approached double the going average, if not higher, arranging among other things a vast expansion of the prison-industrial complex to manage this human surplus. The process of racialization is itself intimately entangled with the production of surplus populations, each functioning to constitute the other according to varying logics of profound exclusion. As Chris Chen argues:

> The rise of the anti-black U.S. carceral state from the 1970s onward exemplifies rituals of state and civilian violence which enforce the racialization of wageless life, and the racial ascription of wagelessness. From the point of view of capital, "race" is renewed not only through persistent racialized wage differentials, or the kind of occupational segregation posited by earlier "split labor market" theories of race, but through the racialization of unwaged surplus or superfluous populations from Khartoum to the slums of Cairo.[22]

This operates in turn at the level of the contemporary riot, a surplus rebellion that is both marked by and marks out race. Hence a final distinction from the strike, which in modern form exists within a legal framework (even if this is often enough exceeded). Here, we begin to understand the kind of ideological work being done by the insistence on the peculiar illegitimacy of riot. The illegality of *riot prime* is among other things the illegality of the racialized body.

---

22   Chris Chen, "The Limit Point of Capitalist Equality," *Endnotes* 3, 2013, 217.

Circulation Struggles

A population, then, whose very being—its possibility for reproduction—is recentered by economic reorganization from the sphere of production into that of circulation. This is not "consumer society" in the popular sense, "the definitive victory of materialism in a universal worship of the commodity-fetish."[23] But it is a consumer society nonetheless: surplus population confronted by the old problem of consumption without direct access to the wage. Not absolutely, not evenly across the globe, but enough. We speak of tendential shifts. When the basis for capital's survival shifts sufficiently to circulation, and the basis for the survival of the immiserated shifts much the same, there we shall find *riot prime*. It thus names the social reorganization, the period in which it holds sway, and the leading form of collective action that corresponds to this situation.

It is a somewhat technical way of talking about exclusion and immiseration, doubtless, this use of categories from classical political economy and its critique. The virtue of this language lies in its power to explain the linkage between *riot* and *riot prime*—to disclose that bread riot and race riot, those paired misnomers, retain a deep unity. In a summary formulation, crisis signals a shift of capital's center of gravity into circulation, both theoretically and practically, and riot is in the last instance to be understood as a circulation struggle, of which price-setting and the surplus rebellion are distinct, though related, forms.

The new proletariat, which must now (in keeping with the original sense of the word) expand to include surplus populations among those "without reserves," finds itself in

---

23   Tom Nairn, "Why It Happened," in *The Beginning of the End: France, May 1968*, eds. Angelo Quattrochi and Tom Nairn, New York: Verso, 1998, 136.

a changed world. We have already detailed some of the changes. The situation can be limned as an epochal chiasmus. In 1700, police as we recognize them did not exist; the occasional bailiff or beadle watched over the marketplace. At the same time, most of life's daily necessities were made locally. In short, the state was far and the economy near. In 2015, the state is near and the economy far. Production is aerosolized; commodities are assembled and delivered across global logistics chains. Even basic foodstuffs are likely to originate a continent away. Meanwhile, the standing domestic army of the state is always at hand— progressively militarized, on the pretext of making war on drugs and terror. *Riot prime* cannot help but heave itself against the state; there is no way not to.

The spectacular encounter with the state should not, however, suggest that there is no directly economic form to the contemporary riot, in addition to its underlying political-economic content. The two manifest forms are economic destruction and looting, one often following on the other in a conjoined negation of market exchange and market logic. Despite the universal appearance of this aspect of the riot, it is unfailingly treated as a deviation from, and compromise of, the initial grievance that might have granted the riot legitimacy. What ethical claim could outright theft possibly make? That this seems at all mysterious points to a moment of ideological closure and supreme historical ignorance. Looting is not the moment of falsehood but of truth echoing across centuries of riot: a version of price-setting in the marketplace, albeit at price zero. It is a desperate turn to the question of reproduction, though one dramatically limited by the structure of capital within which it initially operates.

If the riot raises the question of reproduction, it does so as negation. It stands as the reversal of labor's fate in late modernity. Labor's historical power has rested on a growing productive sector and its ability to seize a share of expanding surplus. Since the turn of the seventies, labor has been reduced to defensive negotiations, compelled to preserve the firms able to supply wages, affirming the domination of capital in return for its own preservation. The worker appearing *as worker* in the period of crisis confronts a situation in which "the very fact of acting as a class appears as an external constraint."[24] This dynamic, which we might call the affirmation trap, has become a generalized social form and conceptual framework, the rational irrationality of our moment. The riot's very disorder can be understood as the immediate negation of this.

Such struggles, in turn, cannot help but confront capital where it is most vulnerable. There is no need to impute a kind of consciousness to this latent form of conflict with capital. Compelled into the space of circulation, the riot finds itself where capital has increasingly shifted its resources. The riot's more or less simultaneous arrival on the freeways of St. Louis, Los Angeles, Nashville, and more than a dozen other cities is as decisive a verdict on the circulation thesis as could be imagined. Easy enough to say that such an interruption is largely symbolic: How much of capital is elsewhere, globally distributed, resilient, dematerialized? The freeway takeovers of late November 2014 are nonetheless an index of the real situation in which struggle will take place. They demonstrate moreover the limits of the various categories of riot. They are self-evidently descendants of the premodern export riots. No less are they siblings to the 2011 port shutdown in Oakland and the

24 Théorie Communiste, "Communization in the Present Tense," in *Communization and its Discontents: Contestation, Critique, and Contemporary Struggles,* ed. Benjamin Noys, New York: Minor Compositions, 2011, 41.

long No-TAV blockade of the planned Susa Valley tunnel. To recognize this is to recognize that the riot is a privileged tactic insofar as it is exemplary of the larger category we designate "circulation struggles": the riot, the blockade, the occupation and, at the far horizon, the commune.

"We are coming to the end of one tradition, and the new tradition has scarcely emerged," Thompson wrote about the transition of two centuries ago.[25] Even the bourgeois press catches a glimpse of this: In 2011, *Newsweek* featured a Tottenham rioter on its cover, tracksuit and mask, flames behind, with the headline THE DECLINE AND FALL OF EUROPE (AND MAYBE THE WEST).[26] Something has ended, or should have ended; everyone can feel it. It is a sort of interregnum. A miserable lull, backlit everywhere by the sense of declension and fires flaring across the planetary terrain of struggle. The songs on the radio are the same—awful, astonishing. They promise that nothing has changed, but they never keep their promises, do they? The fissures in the organization of society that has obtained for some while widen weekly. And yet this anxious persistence, this uneasy suspension. Will there be a restoration? Greater catastrophe? Which should we prefer? This is the tonality of the time of riots.

25 Thompson, "Moral Economy," 128.
26 *Newsweek*, August 22, 2011.

PART 1: RIOT

CHAPTER I

What Is a Riot?

At stake in the definition of riot is not simply the possibility of making useful historical distinctions, but the deciphering of the riot's political significance and potential. It is also a problem for research. Certainly, riots often feature violence, direct, indirect, or threatened. Problems arise once the two are indexed to each other. If one is, for example, parsing public records and selects *violence* and related words for search terms, this indexing will have a profound effect on the results. Just so, the presupposition that violence indicates a riot will instantly present challenges for any useful conceptualization of the activity in question.

Consider the confusions that proliferate once one makes the conflation, in this example from the opening of Gilje's *Rioting in America*:

> Even in the opening years of the nineteenth century, just as workers refined their strike tactics, coercion was needed to enforce unity and to persuade owners of the legitimacy of the laborers' demands. That coercion frequently took the form of rioting—whether it was tarring and feathering a recalcitrant shoemaker in Baltimore, or brawling with strikebreakers on New York docks. Force was often garnered to meet force, and riots and violence represent the signposts of American labor history from the 1830s

to the twentieth century. Before 1865 most violent strikes were limited to cracked heads and were local affairs. After 1865, the rioting became national in scope. In the great railroad strike of 1877 workers fought the military from Baltimore to San Francisco. The dimensions of these labor wars continued to capture national headlines with battles at Homestead in 1892, Pullman in 1894, Ludlow in 1914, and Blair Mountain, West Virginia, in 1921. Add to these major cataclysms countless skirmishes in the cities, towns, and countryside, and we can see that much of the history of American labor is written in blood as riots.[1]

The riot, we are somewhat surprised to learn, is a signal aspect of labor history. It is an adjunct to the strike, its armed wing. Or perhaps riot is simply a subcategory, the *violent strike*; these sometimes rise to the status of "labor wars," eventually arriving at the final, grammatically awkward flourish, determined to place the words "riots" and "blood" in closest possible proximity.

As is often the case with even the most arbitrary concatenations, a truth is nonetheless captured. The echo of "written in letters of blood and fire" is suggestive. Marx's famous description of primitive accumulation insists on the violence of the expropriations producing the conditions of possibility for capitalism. As the chevaliers of industry replace the chevaliers of the sword, it will henceforth appear that the appropriation of surplus under capital, unlike all previous modes of production, is secured through assent freely given. But this double freedom of labor—*from* the means of subsistence, and *to* dispose of one's capacities at will—is precisely what was secured by that originary violence, which is not dissolved, but rather

---

1 Gilje, *Rioting in America*, 3.

sublated and preserved within the impersonal domination of the labor relation.

It can be no wonder, then, that violence stalks the scene of labor. This is the kernel of truth in Gilje's retelling, and the moment in which violence could have been recognized as analytically independent from the constitution of riot. With such a clarifying separation, the ideological force of this exclusive association could come up for inspection. This is precisely what does not happen. It is the character of bourgeois thought to preserve moral rather than practical understanding of social antagonism. So, instead, we encounter the remarkable insistence that violence is always and in every case the sign of riot—even when it involves "brawling with strikebreakers," an evident absurdity. Citing "some legal precedent," Gilje will eventually arrive at his completed definition of riot as "any group of twelve or more people attempting to assert their will immediately through the use of force outside the normal bounds of the law."[2] A riot, we cannot help but notice, is the perfect obverse of a jury.

The riot is, in this telling, always and everywhere illegitimate, which might not surprise us but for the initial claim that it has served "to persuade owners of the legitimacy of the laborers' demands." From there, the categorical problems only proliferate. The consequence of this particular telling is to reduce the strike in its entirety to that most minimal and ascetic aspect, the inaction to be found in the downing of tools. It is always pacific and always within the law—this despite the long stretches of history during which even the meekest strike or "combination" has been illegal, and against the countless examples of picket line struggles and other forms of violence.

---

2   Ibid., 4.

Through such counterfactual constructions, we obtain a gravely narrowed model of strike, both in terms of what actions it might comprise, and its scope historical and geographical. Indeed, the strike contemplated here barely exists at all. Such a definition has as well the contrary effect of broadening and disfiguring our sense of riot beyond any particularity; it is to be found in all times and places as something verging on transhistorical essence. A more persuasive but still limited definition is offered by David Halle and Kevin Rafter:

> [The riot] involves at least one group publicly, and with little or no attempt at concealment, illegally assaulting at least one other group or illegally attacking or invading property ... in ways that suggest that authorities have lost control ... the attacks on another group or on property to reach a certain threshold of intensity.[3]

This might be usefully contrasted with the assessment of William Sewell, one of the foremost historians of collective action. While drawing on Tilly, Sewell, too, gives violence pride of place within his analytic framework across historical periods, concluding, "Tilly's essential argument can still be explicated most economically by using his typology of competitive, reactive, and proactive violence."[4] Where Sewell differs from Gilje is that, by displacing the riot/strike terms onto registers of violence rather than overlaying the two frameworks by force, he is able to reckon the

---

3 David Halle and Kevin Rafter, "Riots in New York and Los Angeles: 1935–2002," in *New York and Los Angeles: Politics, Society, and Culture—A Comparative View,* ed. David Halle, Chicago: University of Chicago Press, 2003, 347.

4 William Sewell, "Collective Violence and Collective Loyalties in France: Why the French Revolution Made a Difference," *Politics and Society,* no.18, 1990, 529.

shift from one leading orientation to another within a repertoire of actions open to historical transformation. That is to say, he retains the possibility of periodizing as such. This is exactly what Gilje effectively abandons by obscuring fully half of the work of history. Tilly notes,

> The repertoire of collective actions evolves in two different ways: the set of means available to people changes as a function of social, economic and political transformations, while each individual means of action adapts to new interests and opportunities for action. Tracing that double evolution of the repertoire is a fundamental task for social history.[5]

The account of riot as the protean expression of general social violence changing form willy-nilly as circumstances dictate informs the second half of this, while effacing the first—and, with it, any chance of grasping the systematic import of the riot's return.

The Economic and the Political

The equivocation of riot and violence has been an essential tool in the political reduction of the riot, its cordoning off from politics proper, the measure of which rests implicitly on a model of self-consciousness or its absence. It was this that Thompson set out to pillory, calling it a "spasmodic view" of popular history:

> According to this view, the common people can scarcely be taken as historical agents before the French Revolution. Before this period, they intrude occasionally in moments of

---

5 Charles Tilly, "Getting It Together in Burgundy, 1675–1975," *Theory and Society*, 4: 4, 1977, 493.

sudden social disturbance. These irruptions are compulsive, rather than self-conscious or self-activating: they are simple responses to economic stimuli.[6]

Such conceptualizations are renewed in the positivistic, quantitative science of, for example, the New England Complex Systems Institute. Their 2011 study, focused on low-wage nations, charts a single-bullet correlation wherein the authors "identify a specific food price threshold above which protests become likely."[7] There are more nuanced departures from these underlying suppositions, articulating unbearable rises in commodity prices with broader economic changes, such as IMF restructuring programs and enforced trade relations, that provide the conditions for precarious food regimes. Emphasizing the constructedness of famine and dearth, these accounts nonetheless assume a veritably autonomous mechanism of enchained stimulus and response. The effective definition of riot here is conditional. It is simply what happens once food prices achieve a certain apogee, a version of the approach by "growth historians" dismissed by Thompson for "obliterating the complexities of motive, behavior, and function, which, if they noted it in the work of their Marxist analogues, would make them protest."[8]

Such an approach finds its counterpoint somewhat perversely in Alain Badiou. He offers an abstracted, qualitative sense of the political moment. In many regards, his account transcends the limits of his contemporaries, left intellectuals who, confronted with the Tottenham riots

6 Thompson, "Moral Economy," 76.
7 Marco Lagi, Karla Z. Bertrand and Yaneer Bar-Yam, "The Food Crises and Political Instability in North Africa and the Middle East," Cambridge, MA: New England Complex Systems Institute, August 10, 2011, 1.
8 Thompson, "Moral Economy," 78.

of 2011, found little to learn. At best, we were given to understand, the riots achieved a sorry spontaneism, that accusation which is socialist thought's reanimation of the "spasmodic" trope. It was an odd spectacle to see a once-modern political theory offered as a truism, as if the debate between Lenin and Luxemburg had been settled and its conclusions were good for all time, no real analysis required. In general, the reports were even less generous. The participants were dupes of the society before them, driven by the self-canceling compulsions of the age, avatars of materialistic individualism momentarily unshackled, perhaps eligible to escape from meaningless outbursts if provided a political program. As Slavoj Žižek inquired plaintively from the paper precincts of the *London Review of Books*, "Who will succeed in directing the rage of the poor?" It was hard not to fear that a philosopher might wish to appoint himself the task.

Badiou, however, is clear that the riots to which he turns his attention are not in search of a vanguard directorate without which they can only affirm the society from which they burst forth. He identifies them as a periodizing fact in the midst of its own realization:

> several peoples and situations are telling us in a still indistinct language that this period is over; that there is a rebirth of History. We must then remember the revolutionary Idea, inventing its new form by learning from what is happening.[9]

The Idea arises from the event of the riot, which it then provides with an organizational force and duration.

In this schema, there is a certain alternation between periods in which "the revolutionary conception of political

---

9   Badiou, *The Rebirth of History*, 87.

action has been sufficiently clarified ... and on this basis has secured massive, disciplined support," and "intervallic periods [when] by contrast, the revolutionary idea of the preceding period ... is dormant."[10] Lacking an ordering idea (often appearing as the majuscule Idea), these latter periods give rise to the expression of that disorder in the protopolitical mode of riot. Badiou sees an "uncanny resemblance" between our recent past and the French Restoration following the final defeat of the Republican spirit: "from the start of the 1830s it was a major period of riots, which were often momentarily or seemingly victorious ... These were precisely the riots, sometimes immediate, sometimes more historical, characteristic of an intervallic period."[11]

The purely economistic and the purely political, as might be expected, display each other's limits in negative. The indexical tale told by the New England Complex Systems Institute can do little but attend to certain quantities as they approach given levels and then await the riot that will inevitably follow. Their method appears to be relatively accurate, after the way of hard data, but it is scarcely explanatory regarding the riot as social phenomenon.

Badiou's recounting, inversely, is admirably explanatory but inaccurate. That is to say, he provides a recognizable social context for riot as opposed to other forms of action, a periodizing claim, and he is prepared to accept the riot as serious testimony about historical transformation. There are nonetheless vagaries in his historical survey, which derives somewhat arbitrary periodizations of French history from imputed political desires, toward a global trajectory of riot to which such a historical apportioning does not correspond. The oscillating movement he educes for France, with phases lasting decades, has little

---

10 Ibid., 38–39.
11 Ibid., 41.

periodizing force; arguably accurate for his native country, it matches little if at all with the tendencies of history elsewhere. Moreover, any given riot of political significance (a "historical riot," in his typology) appears as a practically determinationless event, outside of time. The quants give us too much causality; Badiou too little.

These two approaches stand before us like Scylla and Charybdis, the hard shoals of vulgar economism and the whirlpool of political abstraction. How to navigate between them, between the riot as hunger game and the riot as emanation of a diaphanous structure of political feeling? No doubt, each is in some sense informative but not yet sufficient. If we have stressed periodization, it is first because fundamental and lasting changes within the repertoire of collective action suggest that periodization is possible in forms more thoroughgoing than spasm or oscillation, on both infranational and supranational scales. If the riot looks at periodization, the period in turn peers back at the riot through the dialectical keyhole. It is hard, perhaps impossible, to establish what a riot is without periodization; with it, the riot (and strike as well) can be understood as a set of practices in the face of practical circumstances, with or without an imaginary regarding the reflexive self-awareness of participants on which so many accounts rest.

It is on practice that Thompson founds his analysis. His conclusion aggregates a colloquy of other practices, including blockade, seizure, resale, threat and actual violence against traders and transporters. It is from these, in relation to a customary sense of the cost of staying alive, that he deduces the practice of price-setting as the unifying activity. Thompson has been in turn critiqued for the weight he gives to custom and to the assumed right to weaponize custom that is seized by the crowd. However, the more basic case he builds approaches the inarguable: the case for recognizing that the situation of riot is neither simple hunger nor political "emotion" (as riot had once been called), but rather the domination of the marketplace. If it was "the point at which working people most often felt their exposure to exploitation, it was also the point— especially in rural or dispersed manufacturing districts—at which they could most easily become organized," and was thereby "as much the arena of class war as the factory and mine became in the industrial revolution."[12]

Talk of class war cannot help but threaten a certain reductionism itself. It does not seem, at least in the orthodox sense it has acquired, entirely adequate to the proto-industrial world in question, nor to the present, when class belonging provides no less a limit than a logic for political mobilization. Just so, as our introduction notes, "price-setting of goods in the marketplace" describes only a fraction of the contemporary riot. Thompson, and he is not alone, points toward a way out in a moment of attention to the subject of the riot. He pauses in his survey to remark, "Initiators of the riots were, very often, the women," for the evident reason that "they were also, of course, those most involved in face-to-face marketing, most sensitive to price significancies, most experienced in detecting short-weight or inferior quality."[13]

This is only reasonable, that those excluded in advance from the "patriarchy of the wage"[14] would encounter most keenly the struggle in the marketplace, once subsistence agriculture is undermined and the basic matter of survival is forced into an expanding sphere of exchange. And

---

12 Thompson, "Moral Economy," 134, 120.

13 Ibid., 115; 116

14 Silvia Federici, *Caliban and the Witch: Women, the Body and Primitive Accumulation*, New York: Autonomedia, 2004, 68, 97–100.

this offers us more than a logic of circulation, the sphere of consumption and exchange. It further begets a logic of reproduction as such.

The Dilemma of Reproduction

Social reproduction is always two-sided. From the side of the dispossessed of capital, it is both the sale of labor power and the purchase of what is needed to reproduce that labor power. From the side of capital itself, it is the valorization of commodities in production and the realization of that value in exchange. These are the same activities, evidently enough, seen from different positions. The clearest illustration of reproduction's double character, its contradictory unity, is the so-called *double moulinet* or, in German, *zwickmühle*, a word that English translates as "dilemma."

In the traditional telling of this dilemma, it is a story of labor: of labor power remade and resold for the wage, and of reproductive labor endlessly appropriated toward this process, most commonly as unwaged "women's work." What Thompson catches a glimpse of is that this reproductive work happens not just in the home—kitchen, bedroom,

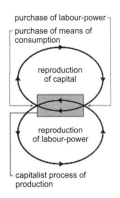

Double moulinet

45

nursery—but is also, in the period he surveys, routed through the marketplace. When the marketplace seems to provide the main situation for reproduction, struggles over reproduction will inevitably situate themselves there. At the same time, we cannot help but notice that this situation does not apply to all subjects equally—that those who are last in and first out of the wage, those who have never been included, those who at best achieve secondary access, will be at the forefront of those who find themselves struggling over reproduction in ways beyond the wage. In this parceling of participants, we encounter another way to see the conjuncture of the eras marked as *riot* and *riot prime*.

In the introduction, we settled on a tripartite definition of *strike* as the form of collective action that struggles to set the price of labor power, is unified by worker identity, and unfolds in the context of production; *riot* struggles to set prices in the market, is unified by shared dispossession, and unfolds in the context of consumption. Strike and riot are distinguished further as leading tactics within the generic categories of production and circulation struggles. We might now restate and elaborate these tactics as being each a set of practices used by people when their reproduction is threatened. Strike and riot are practical struggles over reproduction within production and circulation respectively. Their strengths are equally their weaknesses. They make structured and improvisational uses of the given terrain, but it is a terrain they have neither made nor chosen. The riot is a circulation struggle because both capital and its dispossessed have been driven to seek reproduction there.

If this seems a somewhat technical language for a sensuously laden experience—a dramatic social antagonism charged with danger and fury and desperation and a certain social pleasure—this is only in answer to the conventional dismissals of the riot already encountered, by way of presenting an argument that should not have needed making in the first place. The riot, comprising practices arrayed against threats to social reproduction, cannot be anything but political. This is not to say that the contradiction of reproduction can be resolved within circulation any more than within production. It is in fact the existence of those two spheres, in their unity and contradiction, that guarantees the existence of and gives form to struggles for reproduction. If the vast expansions of the industrial revolution provide the surpluses for the development of modern military and police apparatuses, they also provide surpluses that can be used to purchase social peace. As these surpluses melt away and increasing portions of the population are rendered surplus to the economy in turn, the state turns more and more to coercion as a management style: the social wage of the Keynesian compromise is withdrawn in favor of police occupation of excluded communities.

Police and riot thus come to presuppose each other. The riot comes to know itself through this imbrication. Walking through Hackney during the riots of 2011, past scenes of distress and excitement, past burning trash bins and the detritus of looting, some observers concluded that "a coherent struggle was being waged here … to insist upon respect from the cops, force recognition of a subject where daily grind sees only an abject."[15] The passage points to riot as a necessary relationship with the current structure of state and capital, waged by the abject—by those excluded from productivity. But it also points to the riot's dependence on its antagonist. In the moment, the police appear as necessity and limit.

---

15 "A Rising Tide Lifts All Boats," *Endnotes* 3 2011, 102.

This is the dialectical theme, this dilemma of necessity and limit. The marketplace, the police, circulation. These are not situations where any final overcoming is possible; they are where struggles begin and flourish, desperately.

CHAPTER 2

The Golden Age of Riot

Among the many places one might commence the story, every one bedeviled by the impossibility of arriving at a true beginning, we might look to Bristol and King's Lynn in 1347. It is too early, of course. These events are outliers on the scatterplot of events that have made their way into chronicles. Precursors at best. Perhaps better to start in the sixteenth century, where "food riots did not follow a hoary tradition: the earliest were like furry little mammals overshadowed by the great crashing dinosaurs of peasant and dynastic rebellions and enclosure battles."[1] Or Thompson's eighteenth century, undisputed locus classicus. Tilly, at his most capacious, proposes the brackets 1650–1850. John Bohstedt sees a three-century span in which "Our third century, from the 1740s to c.1820, was the golden age of food riots."[2] Thompson notes these are often identified as "insurrections" or "risings of the poor." Others following Thompson caution against imposing overly rigid distinctions among types, choosing to recommend instead the

---

1   John Bohstedt, *The Politics of Provisions: Food Riots, Moral Economy, and Market Transition in England, c. 1550–1850*, Surrey, UK: Ashgate, 2013, 27.

2   John Bohstedt, "The Pragmatic Economy, the Politics of Provisions and the 'Invention' of the Food Riot Tradition in 1740," in *Moral Economy and Popular Protest: Crowds, Conflicts and Authority*, eds. Adrian Randall and Charles Molesworth, New York: St. Martin's Press, 2000, 57–59.

approach of "moving away from the compartmentaliza-tion of protest. While division of protests into different 'types'—food, industrial, political, customary, and so on—may be neater, it obscures our understanding of the very linkages which overarched them."[3]

The linkage is linkage itself: exchange as social synthe-sis. Marx remarks that "the simplest economic category, say e.g. exchange value, presupposes population, moreover a population producing in specific relations." It is with this that "the bringing of the product to market ... could more precisely be regarded as the transformation of the product *into a commodity.* Only on the market is it a *commodity.*"[4]

The rise of markets in the abstract sense is inevitably uneven across space and in time, and often hard to see. Nonetheless, the food riot rises with the market en route to becoming the paradigmatic form of social conflict. "As a growing mass of workers came to depend on markets for their food, England became increasingly vulnerable to harvest failure and to food riots," Bohstedt notes.[5] Tilly says about France, "We have noticed the durable rise of the food riot at the end of the seventeenth century, as the pressure on communities to surrender local grain reserves to the demands of the national market increased."[6] Richard Price, taking up Thompson's framework: "Price riots and struggles over rationalized use of land were characteris-tic forms of this clash between the innovations of market forces and the assertion of a 'moral economy' of reciprocal obligations and responsibilities."[7]

---

3   Adrian Randall and Charles Molesworth, "The Moral Eco-nomy: Riots, Markets, and Social Conflict," in *Moral Economy and Popular Protest: Crowds, Conflicts and Authority,* 12.
4   Marx, *Grundrisse,* 101, 534 (emphasis in original).
5   Bohstedt, "Pragmatic Economy," 57.
6   Tilly, "Burgundy," 503.
7   Richard Price, *Labour in British Society: An Interpretive*

The question of "moral economy" leans heavily on the significance of particular self-recognitions on the part of the antagonists. In this it is exemplary of much thought regarding riot, an explanatory device relying on intention and *ratio* as a bulwark against depoliticizing analyses, counterposing self-reflexity to mere reflex. It is Thompson at his most justificatory, when justification is not necessarily the task at hand. One historian counterposes a "pragmatic economy," arguing, "If food riots and moral economy/paternalistic beliefs were as entrenched in defense of tradition as Thompson argued, those traditions and beliefs ought to have been manifest in the first national waves of riots in 1740, 1756–57 and 1766."[8] However, "It will be clear by now that the rioters of 1740 were more interested in seizing food than regulating markets."[9]

Seizing food and regulating markets are opposed only in the realm of ideology. As both sides seem to miss here, the moral sense of the crowd (should such a thing exist) is an instrument of pragmatic needs, not their contravention. The cause of the event lies elsewhere, in social transformation. Once the market is generalized and exchange becomes, in the terms of Alfred Sohn-Rethel, a "second, purely social nature" set next to the first nature of use—once reproduction itself is hemmed all around—price cannot but become a site of immediate antagonism.

But we should not lean too heavily on the magic of "price." To insist on the distinction is to neglect that the zero of seizure is a price, too; it stands in relation to the total funds available to meet basic needs. Within the context of the market, direct expropriation finds itself on the same continuum of a redistributive struggle for survival as does

---

History, London: Croom Helm, 1968, 29.

8 Bohstedt, "Pragmatic Economy," 75.

9 Ibid., 67.

demanding a lower cost of grain. Tilly makes this point himself about England, France, and the eventual United States:

> During the period from 1650 to 1850, people most often either kept grain from leaving town by seizing the shipment or forced local food into the market at a price lower than the owner preferred. The authorities called those actions food riots, but in fact they consisted of ordinary people's doing almost exactly what the authorities themselves commonly did in time of shortage—forbid grain from leaving town, commandeer local supplies, regulate the price.[10]

Seizing food *is* market regulation, much as exporting food in the midst of dearth is market regulation.

The World Market

It is for this reason that we begin at the docks. In 1347, there are two notable riots in England, at the Hanseatic League ports of Bristol and King's Lynn:

> Once on board, the crowd, assuming royal power, unloaded the ships "against the will of the owners" and put the grain up for sale "at their own price." The protestors also seized and sold other shipments of corn being brought into Lynn to be marketed and then "on their authority" sentenced the owners or carriers to the pillory, "without process of law." Finally, the crowd was accused of arresting the mayor and other inhabitants and issuing quasi-royal proclamations.[11]

---

10 Tilly, "Speaking Your Mind," 470.
11 Buchanan Sharp, "The Food Riots of 1347 and the Medieval Moral Economy," in *Moral Economy and Popular Protest: Crowds, Conflicts and Authority*, eds. Adrian Randall and Charles Molesworth, New York: St. Martin's Press, 2000, 35–35.

This carnival assumption of power haunts the riot; more than four centuries later, the Gordon Riots will sign the breached wall of Newgate Prison, "His Majesty, King Mob." After a point, command over price is not so easy to distinguish from sovereignty. But it is a different fact that is most telling here. In Bristol's port the ships are bound for Gascony, those leaving from King's Lynn for Bordeaux. The world market is in formation, a project of merchants, militaries, banks. The events at Bristol and King's Lynn follow shortly after England defaults on the massive loans from Florence with which it financed the invasion of France; both Gascony and Bordeaux are hinges of the Hundred Years' War. The trading network of the Mediterranean propagates this volatility, the "great crash" of the 1340s (featuring the first banking collapse, taking down the Houses of Bardi and Peruzzi). Against this drama within the nascent world-system, the export riots of 1347 play but a minor role.[12] Nonetheless they are woven into its tapestry, warp and weft.

The port, the entrepôt, even on a limited scale (for what is King's Lynn compared to Venice in the High Middle Ages, or to seventeenth-century Amsterdam?) is as close as the made world will come to the intersection in theory of production and circulation. If it is the hurly-burly of the local market writ large, it is at the same time the condensation

---

12 It is worth noting here that "world-system" is not intended to designate the entirety of the globe and then treat Western Europe as if it could play that role in analysis as it so often does in western imaginations. As Immanuel Wallerstein clarifies, "Putting in the hyphen was intended to underline that we are not talking about systems, economies, empires of the (whole) world, but about systems, economies, empires *that are* a world (but quite possibly, and indeed usually, not encompassing the entire globe)." Immanuel Wallerstein, *World-Systems Analysis: An Introduction*, Durham: Duke University Press, 2004, 16–17.

of all the abstractions of world space, commercial arrangements, portulans, admiralty law. It is the built landscape where the relation of the local and the global is on display. Outside the port, it is hard to reconcile the two, if one has not traveled much: the quotidian civic doings of the agora and the notional sublime of oceanic trade. It is the distance between the ledger book and adventure fiction. Franco Moretti observes,

> Adventures make novels long because they make them wide; they are the great explorers of the fictional world: battlefields, oceans, castles, sewers, prairies, islands, slums, jungles, galaxies ... Margaret Cohen, from whom I have learned a lot on this, sees it as a trope of expansion: capitalism on the offensive, planetary, crossing the oceans. I think she is right, and would only add that the reason adventure works so well within this context is that it's so good at imagining *war*.[13]

From this perspective, the achievement of *Robinson Crusoe* is to synthesize ledger book and adventure—to discover among the truths that modernity will put on offer the unity of the two. As Marx has it, "so does private exchange create world trade, private independence creates complete dependence on the so-called world market."[14] Walter Raleigh's aphorism precedes this: "All trade is world trade; all world trade is maritime trade." A dialectic of merchant's stall and world market then, the entanglement of the most local and farthest-flung phenomena. And along with this, the dialectic of riot and war, King's Lynn and Calais, each at a far end of a shared skein.

---

13 Franco Moretti, "The Novel: History and Theory," *New Left Review*, no. 52, July–August 2008, 115, 124.
14 Marx, *Grundrisse*, 159.

It matters little, to return to an earlier theme, whether the rioters possess thoughts of world markets, distant conflicts, the tightening mesh of global space. They have a practical task that arises within these, from these, and takes part in them regardless. The participants cannot stop turning toward these things, which haunt every horizon. Thompson, discussing the overlooked planning and patience of the marketplace riot in all its local particularity, is drawn by the magnetic pull of export:

> Moreover, they required more preparation and organization than is at first apparent; sometimes the "mob" controlled the marketplace for several days, waiting for prices to come down; sometimes actions were preceded by hand-written (and, in the 1790s, printed) handbills; sometimes the women controlled the marketplace, while parties of men intercepted grain on the roads, at the docks, on the rivers; very often the signal for action was given by a man or woman carrying a loaf aloft, decorated with black ribbon, and inscribed with some slogan.[15]

Here, the common sense of riot's history becomes a narration, in which the export riot is a sort of digression, a substory. It is finally of great significance in tracing the long historical arc of riot to understand that this has matters reversed. Let us consider the century of national riot waves. In 1740, the strong majority are "crowd action

---

15 E. P. Thompson, *The Making of the English Working Class*, Vintage Books, 1966, 65. He goes on to footnote J. F. Sutton, *The Date-Book of Nottingham*, Nottingham, 1880 edn., p. 286: "A Nottingham action in September 1812 commenced with several women, sticking a half penny loaf on the top of a fishing rod, after having streaked it with red ochre, and tied around it a shred of black crape, emblematic ... of 'bleeding famine decked in Sackecloth.' " The red and black flag begins in bread.

to stay transport of food." They cluster around coasts and waterways: the mouths of the Thames and the Severn, King's Lynn, along the Ouse and even the Union Canal. The more widespread riots of 1756–1757 see an increase both in explicit price-setting and attacks on dealers, but still tilt toward transport; they cluster again around waterways and toward the Midlands. Around 1795, Thompson's "climactic year" for riot, underwritten by famine and channeled Jacobinism, riots are to be found everywhere below Northumberland; price-setting now equals transport. There is no shortage of either. By 1800–1801, it is riots one piled on the next, spreading throughout the Midlands and spanning the southern coast in a last peak before riot begins to decline in England.[16] And not in England alone; the course is much the same in the North American colonies, where the exemplary rioters of 1709 through 1713 attacked ships, in one case snapping a rudder against the departure of a shipment of wheat; these events are intimately tied to emerging West Indian trade.

The pattern is perfectly clear. The export riot, the direct physical intervention into transport, is scarcely a divergence or improvisation within the trajectory of riot, but rather its baseline. It is there at the origin, an invention of emerging national and international markets, financing of the national purse, the commoditization of agriculture, and the corresponding destruction of communal self-sufficiency. From its earliest beginnings, the riot has been a quintessential circulation struggle. Even the most discrete and rustic seditions have shared this expansive context. After 1521, there began an even more dramatic and blood-dimmed expansion, the catastrophe of colonization, slavery, spice routes—what some historians will call

16   Andrew Charlesworth, ed., *An Atlas of Rural Protest in Britain 1548–1900*, London: Croom Helm, 1983, 81, 84, 98, 102.

"the first globalization," the mercantilist era that integrates the world economy in the span between the voyages of Columbus and Da Gama at one end and the Industrial Revolution at the other. That this mercantilist era more or less matches the first age of riots is not a telling correlation, but the riot's historical and theoretical basis.

Riot and Class Struggle

In the riot's first blossoming are the seeds of its decline. England centers the early part of this study not because it is the first home to riot but because it is home to the first transition, *riot-strike*. The logic of riot stands out most starkly in contrast. The next chapter is given over to this transition. However, the underlying dynamics of that transition are already emergent during the golden age of riot. In a self-canceling and self-propelling movement that we must by now find familiar, this emergence is both the condition for that golden age and for what will bring the age to an end.

The development of the market coincides with increasing pressure on population across Europe beginning in the late fifteenth century and a concomitant rise in grain prices. In these conditions, according to Brenner's persuasive account of the rise of capitalism in England, "we find the landlords consolidating holdings and leasing them out to large capitalist tenants who would in turn farm them on the basis of wage labor and agricultural improvement."[17] In France this process is inhibited by the state's inclination to protect peasant tenure. Two different developmental paths result, eloquently assessed by Ellen Meiksins Wood:

---

17 Robert Brenner, "Agrarian Class Structure and Economic Development in Pre-Industrial Europe," *Past and Present*, no. 70, February 1976, 61.

the dynamic of self-sustaining growth, and the constant need for improvement of labor productivity, presupposed transformations in property relations that created a need for such improvements simply to permit the principal economic actors—landlords and peasants—to reproduce themselves. The divergences between England and France, for example, had little to do in the first instances in their respective technological capacities. They were distinguished by the nature of relations between landlords and peasants: one case demanded enhancement of labor-productivity, the other did not and in some ways even impeded the development of productive forces. The systematic drive to revolutionize the forces of production was result more than cause.[18]

Small-peasant production could be intensified, and often was. However, this was generally done through increased labor. This was scarcely an escape from the Malthusian trap, and as Brenner notes, it depended on greater basic grain production elsewhere:

> English economic development thus depended upon a nearly unique symbiotic relationship between agriculture and industry. It was indeed, in the last analysis, an agricultural revolution, based on the emergence of capitalist class relations in the countryside which made it possible for England to become the first nation to experience industrialization.[19]

These different paths dictate different struggles:

---

18 Ellen Meiksins Wood, *The Origin of Capitalism: A Longer View*, London: Verso, 2002, 66–7.
19 Brenner, "Agrarian Class Structure," 68.

In England, of course, peasant revolt was directed against the landlords, in a vain last-ditch struggle to defend disintegrating peasant proprietorship against advancing capitalist encroachment. In France the target of peasant revolt was, typically, the crushing taxation of the absolutist state.[20]

Here, Brenner refers to peasant uprisings such as Kett's Rebellion in 1549, the largest of the period's enclosure riots. As noted earlier, these are related to food riots by the question of subsistence, but that is a wide net. We might refine this via the suggestion that the peasant uprising is an uncle to what we will eventually recognize as the riot, a feudal stand against restructuring that slowly surrenders its force as its world unevenly fades away. The riot survives after its older relative has passed into memory. But for some time it develops alongside.

This is to be expected. The market, the world of exchange and consumption, has a long history. It is this fact that led Fernand Braudel to claim that the economy has three layers. Daily life provides the ground layer, with the market above that. "Then alongside, or rather above this layer, comes the zone of the anti-market, where the great predators roam and where the law of the jungle operates."[21] What this misses is the way in which capitalism is not simply an added layer but also a social relation that transforms the content of the market it finds before it while at first preserving its form (increasingly doing the same with daily life). Now it will be where value is realized, behind the scrim of buying cheap and selling dear. Capitalism is the internalization of commerce, not its other: a capitalism

---

20 Ibid., 70.

21 Fernand Braudel, *The Wheels of Commerce: Civilization and Capitalism, Fifteenth–Eighteenth Century, Vol. 2*, Berkeley: University of California Press, 1982, 230.

at first merchant-based, circulatory. And the period when this process of internalization is in full churn—after the agricultural revolution begins, before the industrial revolution takes hold—this will be the golden age of riot.

CHAPTER 3

The Swing, Or, Riot to Strike

It is impossible, surely, to discover the exact moment when strike overtakes riot in the repertoire. Any such determination would be overconfident about the clarity and punctuality with which forms of struggle develop, diverge, reform. Worse still would be to suggest that one vanishes, to be replaced by the other. Tactics once they are adopted are always at hand, nearer or farther.

Moreover, in seeking the transition, we have the difficulty already set forth. The shift from riot to strike is immanent to a more thoroughgoing and complex shift in the structure of capital ascendant. The strike emerges from the riot—from a mode centered by profit-taking in the market to one centered by surplus-value extraction. That is to say, the strike emerges into the new world of capitalist production, as it must, from the space of circulation. It strides from the sea trailing foam, if not yet quite fully formed. British, American, and French sailors were consistently among the most militant workers in the eighteenth century, rivaling shoemakers (the tradesmen found most consistently among leaders of political disturbances from the seventeenth century through the Paris Commune). The English word *strike* itself seems to date from 1768, when sailors joined "city artisans and tradesmen—weavers, hatters, sawyers, glass-grinders, and coal heavers—in the fight for better wages, [and] struck their sails and paralyzed the city's commerce. They 'unmanned or otherwise prevented from sailing every ship in the Thames.' "[1]

The derivation of the French term for strike, *grève*, is even more suggestive—an etymology with the reach of an epic, beginning on a riverbank and ending at the Hôtel de Ville a few centuries later and eighty paces away. It is an old word. Originally it meant a flat area of sand and gravel next to the water, a strand, and so a place where boats unloaded cargo. The most workable *grève* on the Seine became therefore the main port of Paris.[2]

It was on the right bank, once the city expanded out from the islands in the river. The open area next to the strand would serve as the city's central market in the High Middle Ages before the stallkeepers decamped for Les Halles. Unskilled laborers would gather there in search of work, loading and unloading wood and wheat, wine barrels and hay bales: the *Place de Grève*. The name would last more than 500 years. In 1802, the square became the *Place de l'Hôtel de Ville*, renamed for its main edifice, the home of the mayor, the Thermidorean coup, and, for a brief time, the Commune. Early photographs show that the Communards raised barricades there in part from great

---

1 Greg Grandin, *The Empire of Necessity: Slavery, Freedom, and Deception in the New World,* New York: Metropolitan Books, 2014, n. 146. The unattributed quotation is from *The Economic Review*, Vol. 5, London: Rivington, Percival & Co., 1895, 216.

2 Eric Hobsbawm makes a fascinating point in *The Age of Revolution: Europe 1789–1848*, London: Abacus, 2007, 265, fn. 31. He writes: "The strike is so spontaneous and logical a consequence of the working-class existence that most European languages have independent native words for it (e.g. *grève, huelga, sciopero, zabastovka*), whereas words for other institutions are often borrowed." However, this is ultimately misleading in ways that will be explored in the following chapter, notably for the ways it declares the strike's autonomy from an older tradition, as if it had arisen autochthonously from the new proletarian dispensation.

wine barrels. A medieval rhyme. Where the market was, the commune will be.

But we are getting ahead of ourselves. We are down at the port once more, the place that provides the main coordinate for this first section, for the golden age of riot. It is inevitable, because it is practically and logically necessary, that port and market midwife the strike. It is equally inevitable, then, that we will return to the port later in this book, as things swing back from strike to riot. It is a catchment of unused labor amid the great machine of the market. A place of misery and possibility. It is fitting, perhaps, that the *Place de Grève* will also host a guillotine; the 1835 dictionary associates the word *grève* with executions. It does not yet mention labor actions.

But the change is already afoot. The rise of capital refines not a few phrases. Chateaubriand, ultra-rightist and inveterate coiner of terms, uses *gréviste* in 1821; for the moment, it does not quite mean a striker, but rather one who opposes the royalists. His nose for politics is sharp as ever. As the bodies gather in the *Place*, the unemployed who will be the first army of the June Days, "*être en grève*" comes to mean "searching for work." By 1848, following an economic collapse along the length of Europe, "*mettre un patron en grève*" signifies "refusing to work for the boss." The modern sense and the modern strike have arrived. The transition is complete.

France arrives there somewhat later than England or the United States for reasons already discussed. The years 1848–1851 are the great pivot, for all their farcical nature. Industrialization will now remake French society at a profound level. Before this passage, puzzlements abound, as they have elsewhere. In 1830, we find "a riot of textile workers occurred in Roubaix; they wanted a raise in pay." The prosecutor from Douai reports, "They broke the windows in the main shops, where they went in force to ask for written agreements about the raise." Roubaix had been a textile center since the late Middle Ages, with well-developed labor organization. Shorter and Tilly record this correctly (if ambiguously) as a prelude to the strike in France, remarking that "sometimes workers in one shop walked off the job for a while, and sometimes they tried to get work stoppages in other shops of the same industry," but more commonly, "the core of their action was a show of strength coupled with the presentation of collective demands concerning the conditions of employment in a particular set of shops. The law of the time forbade almost any sort of collective action by workers."[3]

The prosecutor clearly has no language for this. The contents of the very social dispensation in which he is enmeshed are not yet known to him: the arrival onto the stage of the laboring classes. He is stuck on the form. It is an angry mob, after all, even if they are workers mobilizing as workers at their place of employ, demanding better pay. The consequence of this formalism is manifest. "The riot, according to my deputy's report, does not appear to have any political overtones," concludes our chronicler. We might suspect that he means the events are not directly related to the July Revolution, two weeks earlier. At the same time, we recognize a common sense on its way to becoming a sleight-of-rhetoric. It does a certain kind of work, this confusion, this peculiar naming habit. *Because* we can name it as a riot, we can proceed as if its manifest political significance does not exist. One more spasm in the historyless history of the immiserated.

---

3   All extracts are from Edward Shorter and Charles Tilly, *Strikes in France 1830–1968,* London: Cambridge University Press, 1984, 1.

Machine-Breaking

"TO THE LABOURING CLASSES," as handbills once began:

> The Gentlemen, Yeomanry, Farmers, and others, having made known to you their intention of increasing your Wages to a satisfactory extent; and it having been good Sense that it will be most beneficial to your own permanent Interests to return to your usual honest occupations, and to withdraw yourselves from practices which tend to destroy the Property from whence the very means of your additional Wages are to be supplied.[4]

This particular posting comes from Berkshire's magistrates; only two English counties handed down more death sentences to "Swing riot" participants, and none imprisoned so many. It is meant to soothe the real followers of the mythical Captain Swing during the wave of machine-breaking begun in the fall of 1830. In the event of it, the Swing riots would last into the next year. The laboring classes at this point are still plural, the fractions set loose by the wreck of feudalism, still in process of being forged into "the working class." Thompson reckons 1790–1832 as the crucible, wherein we find as well that more durable episode of machine-breaking, the Luddite uprisings of 1811–1813.

Over and over, Swing is about threshing machines. Equally, "Luddite attacks were confined to particular industrial objectives: the destruction of power-looms (Lancashire), shearing-frames (Yorkshire), and resistance

---

4 Eric Hobsbawm and George Rude, *Captain Swing: A Social History of the Great English Agricultural Uprising of 1830*, New York: W. W. Norton, 1968, 136.

to the breakdown of custom in the Midland framework-knitting industry."[5]

We have encountered already the drive-train, which, turned by agrarian advances, will spin the wheels of the Industrial Revolution. The race for productivity, the very basis of capitalist development, means the replacement of labor power with means of production, living labor with dead, variable capital with constant. Increasing productivity tends to increase wages, which in turn forces further labor-saving advances. In parallel, masses of in-servants are thrown onto the labor market: rising costs of agricultural produce persuade employers to abandon residual work-in-kind arrangements for wages, passing on inflation to workers. The agrarian labor loosed by enclosure depresses those same wages even as industry strides the landscape in seven-league boots.

As the wage generalizes itself, the marketplace begins to surrender its social centrality. The physical space subject in part to communal control gives way to "the mysteries of a 'self-regulating' market, the price mechanism, and the subordination of all communal values to the imperative of profit."[6] Shortly, "the characteristic member of the rural poor was now a landless proletarian, relying almost exclusively on wage-labor or on the Poor Law for his or her living."[7] The Poor Law is a reminder, in light of previous discussions, that zero is a wage, too, though one that will need supplement if its recipients are to be kept in available reserve.

Amid this arise General Ludd and Captain Swing, one leading sallies against the textile industries, the other in the agrarian theater of combat. Both movements described

---

5 Thompson, *Working Class*, 484.
6 Wood, *Origin of Capitalism*, 69.
7 Hobsbawm and Rude, *Captain Swing*, 35.

themselves in military terms, never better than in a letter "Signed by the General of the Army of Redressers Ned Ludd Clerk." They took oaths, stocked arms. Sustained and popular, that they were real uprisings can scarcely be debated. Their spans were various. They had no single activity. In the Swing riots alone, "arson, threatening letters, 'inflammatory' handbills and posters, 'robbery,' wages meetings, assaults on overseers, parsons and landlords, and the destruction of different types of machinery all played their part." For all this variability of form, the content is steady. "Behind these multiform activities, the basic aims of laborers were singularly consistent: to attain a minimum living wage and to end rural unemployment."[8] No less clear were the Luddites, whose "demands included a legal minimum wage; the control of the 'sweating' of women or juveniles; arbitration; the engagement by the masters to find work for skilled men made redundant by machinery; the prohibition of shoddy work; the right to open trade union combination."[9]

We should not suggest that the two great episodes of machine-breaking are identical. Their grounds are different. For all their linkage, the agricultural and industrial worlds in Great Britain are at odds; the obdurate battles over the Corn Laws underscore the contrary interests of country and town. Kirkpatrick Sale titles his study *Rebels Against the Future: The Luddites and Their War on the Industrial Revolution*; could one say the same of the Swing rioters?[10] But it is misleading, if in keeping with half of Thompson's spirit, to reckon the revolts as backward-facing defenses

---

8 Ibid., 195.

9 Thompson, "Working Class," 551.

10 Kirkpatrick Sale, *Rebels Against the Future: The Luddites and Their War on the Industrial Revolution: Lessons for the Computer Age*, Boston: Addison-Wesley, 1995.

of custom. Again we confront the question of the practical, of necessity. Often enough the Luddites put matters in ways hard to mistake, affirming their right and intention to "break and destroy all manner of frames whatsoever that do not pay the regular price heretofore agreed." A list is attached to this communiqué; machines that displace no workers will be left intact.[11] Ludd and Swing doubtless share a sense of dangerously shifting ground, of a life-world under duress. Yet they are conjoined, in the minimal formula, by downward pressure on wages and the threat of technological unemployment. And it is here that the puzzle of classification asserts itself.

Officials, predictably, wish to grant them insurrectionary force only when necessary to levy increased penalties. For the most part the great episodes of machine-breaking will be recorded as riots by observers, at the time and later. After all, laws give names, and often enough it is the crime of riot for which the armies of Ludd and Swing are prosecuted (though a specific bill rendering frame-breaking a capital crime will be passed early on). Nottingham magistrates report "an outrageous spirit of tumult and of riot" in the early days of Ludd, setting forth the terms of art for Riot Act convictions.

Occasionally the name seems fitting, for example applied to the forcing of money and provisions. The actual episodes, for all their variety, often resemble the riot formally—in their tone, momentum, wildness. And yet. It should be impossible to look at those demands and not recognize the strike in formation. They concern only employment, better wages, better working conditions, legal protections. If we are searching for the wellspring of the great confusion between the underlying nature of collective struggle

---

11   Conant and Darval, quoted in Thompson, "Working Class," 535.

and its appearance, we need look no further than these events.

Let us make the argument clearly, not least because it is an argument about confusion. It is only within this period of historical transition that the contours of riot and strike can stand finally clear in their delineations, exactly because it is only in such periods that the two can be placed in such close quarters, admixed, and in the end clarified. Or to put this another way, machine-breaking is what the swing from riot to strike looks like. No doubt it looks backward, "the last chapter of a story which begins in the 14th and 15th centuries."[12] But this insistence on custom, on the fight against the future, misses that part of machine-breaking that is invention, which anticipates. It is no less a first chapter of confrontational workplace politics that have not ended. It is only in a period of transition that such a shocking and novel hybrid, one foot in enclosure and food riots, one foot in factory legislation and struggles over the working day, might arise. "We are coming to the end of one tradition, and the new tradition has scarcely emerged," writes Thompson.[13] In such a circumstance it is inevitable that tactics will proliferate as people try solutions to a new set of problems, borrowing their forms from the old repertoire—just as capital draws its forms from commerce until the new content is ready to go forth by day.

It is precisely the transition from marketplace to workplace, from the price of goods to the price of labor power as the fulcrum of reproduction, that dictates the swing from riot to strike in the repertoire of collective action. In fact, these are the same, context and conflict. They move together. The close rhythm of this double change provides the historical ground for a political-economic argument

---

12   Thompson, "Working Class," 543.
13   Thompson, "Moral Economy," 128–9.

that defines riot and strike adequately in their historical fullness—defines them not according to given activities but rather to the ways that the problem of reproduction confronts the mass of people, their positions within the given social relations, the places where they have been pushed, the spaces where their antagonists must be visible, might be vulnerable.

The Many

> Rise, like lions after slumber,
> In unvanquishable number,
> Shake your chains to earth like dew
> Which in sleep had fallen on you—
> Ye are many—they are few—
>
> —Percy Bysshe Shelley,
> "The Masque of Anarchy"

If one went searching for a red thread running through the sequence *riot-strike-riot prime,* one could do worse than to follow the fate of Shelley's poem, composed for "a little volume of *popular songs* wholly political."[14] The poem narrates the Peterloo Massacre of 1819, named with some irony after Waterloo, fought four years earlier. It is the middle of Thompson's crucible, then. England is in famine and depression. The food riot, having peaked by all accounts in 1800–1, is in retreat. The end of the Napoleonic wars has thrown a great mass of bodies onto a labor market unable to absorb them. Indigency in England stands at 15 percent, and emigration at historical highs.

---

14   Letter to Leigh Hunt, May 1, 1820, *The Letters of Percy Bysshe Shelley: In Two Vols.*, vol. 2, ed. Frederick L. Jones, Oxford: Clarendon Press, 1964, 191 (emphasis in original).

It is against this backdrop that 60,000 gather in St. Peter's Field in Manchester seeking parliamentary reforms, mostly regarding suffrage. The Riot Act is read. In the cavalry charge immediately following, more than a dozen demonstrators are killed, hundreds wounded. Moral outrage seizes the nation. In Italy, Shelley constructs his poem from newspaper reports.

It would be hard to name Peterloo itself a riot in the sense the word had developed over the preceding centuries. It is close in certain ways. The great assembly gathers in the agora. The term and the legal code are used in any case; it is the representational category people have to hand. Certainly there were gatherings that can more properly be called riots over the following days in surrounding cities. But the eighteenth-century riot has in main reached its limit and burst. The mass gathering in the square will tilt toward revolution or nothing, pressed against the impossibility of the practical demand when even calls for reform are met with deadly violence. This is where the poem begins. The shift away from riot has already begun. James Chandler writes,

> All this is to say that Peterloo-like "the French Revolution" on a higher scale or perhaps even "Romanticism" itself on a scale yet higher still—names an event of indeterminate duration that marks a major transformation in the practices of modern literary and political representation, one understood in its moment to have revolutionary potential.[15]

But the poem is not published until 1832, at the far end of our first swing. The final stanza of the long poem will

---

15 James Chandler, *England in 1819: The Politics of Literary Culture and the Case of Romantic Historicism*, Chicago: University of Chicago Press, 1998, 18.

become a kind of marching song for struggle after struggle. It is taken up shortly by the Chartists, who in 1842 lurch close to the first general strike. The time of labor has begun. In 1911, Pauline Newman will orient her organizing speeches for the International Ladies' Garment Worker's Union with Shelley's phrases. But there will be further swings. In 2010, the poem is repatriated when students and others fighting fatal cuts to the social wage storm and occupy 30 Millbank, the Conservative Party headquarters in London. Shelley's final stanza is cited repeatedly in the following days, the red thread returning in the long season that includes the movement of the squares, the Occupy movement, the Arab Spring—the return of the riot.

The final stanza adds a last line to a quatrain appearing earlier, glancing away from the poem's bedrock pacifism: "Ye are many—they are few."[16] It might be possible to persuade you that the sounds in the first line, *rise/lions/after*, want you to hear the word *riot*. It is hard not to. It is hard not to hear in the poem's association of "Anarchy" with the corrupt state rather than with the state's antagonists a precursor to the dialectical inversion with which we began this book: "A violent order is a disorder; and A great disorder is an order. These two things are one." But Shelley's last line asks a simpler or perhaps far more intractably complex question, that of *the many*.

The popular and the political, as he insisted. Crowds and power, in Canetti's pithy formula. Masses, classes, mob, multitude. Subjects, citizens, the people. The sense of social antagonism and metamorphosis, the sense of (to risk that portentous substantialization) *the political*: This cannot be extricated from the sense of *the many*, and what it is that might give them a unity, be it self-declared or spectral. This

---

16 Different printings of the poem vary in their orthography; this citation follows the first edition, London: Edward Moxon, 1832.

is hardly the place for a survey of the literature. Instead, a simple proposition: that *riot* and *strike* have served as, among other things, metonyms for this matter within a given moment.

This is another way to limn what is grasped in the idea of a repertoire of collective action and of identifying a lead tactic within it. These tactics, and the changes among them, are expressions of the social mass and its recompositions, which in turn form and transform from given material bases. To put this otherwise, the riot is not an isolated and singular event; it is both a real fraction of and a figure for *the many* to which it is always adjacent. It is the many's internal relation externalized under certain conditions. This is true of the strike as well. To understand the transformations in the sequence *riot-strike-riot prime* is to see into the changes of the many, see what might be comprehended in them.

PART 2: STRIKE

CHAPTER 4

Strike Contra Riot

What kind of other is the strike to the riot? The nineteenth century sets itself to this measure, to the figuring of the relationship. It does so unevenly across western Europe, Great Britain, the United States—insistently, uncertainly, but with consequential results.

This book is not a history of the strike or the labor movement, of the era in which proletarianization denotes agrarian dispossession, industrial expansion, absolute and relative increase of global entrance into the wage, and individual sovereignty as the mode of integration into circuits of accumulation. Nonetheless, these are coordinates of the period into which the golden age of riots dissolves, and from which the new era of riots emerges: the long Monday of the world in which it was always time for work and productive capitalism ran the table on a global scale, in its volatile fashion.

The strike, the dominant tactic of collective action in this period, will want some reckoning—not least because the status of the strike, once it becomes the leading figure for social antagonism, offers a position from which to reflect on the riot. Each action clarifies the structure and dynamic of the other, each betrays changes within the lurching, subterranean metamorphoses of capital. This is true not just in some absolute way according to which the truth of each can be contrasted, but also according to political conceptions of the pair and of the pairing—what we might call ideologies of riot and strike.

In the previous chapter, we proposed the broadest possible understanding of a strike: a struggle over the price of labor power and over employment itself, conducted by workers as workers in the sphere of production. These features might be abstracted and extended to any action oriented by them. This strike arrives early, coexisting with the riot as it gathers its powers.

This is obviously overbroad. A thought experiment, let's say. Certainly it is at odds with conventional understandings developed since the nineteenth century, which offer a far narrower gate through which a tactic must pass to earn the name. The narrow strike is generally defined according to a self-naming or self-recognition, which must be coupled with a particular bodily and political comportment: orderly, anchored in place, disciplined, legalistic, characterized by refusal. Forms of appearance, in short, that might be discerned by a casual observer. If an episode fails or exceeds these standards, it is deemed not to be a strike. (We might think of the Coal Field Strikes of 1913–1914, which at some point in the concerted series of strikes became the Colorado Coalfield War and then the Ludlow Massacre.) Or, as happens over and over, the events that do not correspond to this model of the strike are effaced so that the name *strike* can preserve its claims. Who now recalls as strikes the risings of Lyon textile workers in 1831 and 1834, which demanded wages, work, and justice for jailed leaders by way of barricades and guerilla fighting? This strike arrives late. The transition period is much longer. Except, as we shall see, there is no transition at all.

Marx himself notes that 1830 marks the shift in France from a state of landlords to one of capitalists. Hobsbawm generalizes the date as a turning point for "working-class consciousness" in the home countries of the two bourgeois and industrial revolutions, a new situation that "certainly came into existence between 1815 and 1848." For him, "in Britain and Western Europe in general [1830] dates the beginning of those decades of crisis in the development of the new society which conclude with the defeat of the 1848 revolutions and the gigantic economic leap forward after 1851.[1]

The temporality there is complex but gets at the belatedness of the strike in its narrow sense. By general agreement, the strike does not have any real existence up to 1830 or in truth for a good while after. Shorter and Tilly are the partial exception. *Strike* does not appear in the index of *The Making of the English Working Class*. John Rule's careful study of English labor from 1750 to 1850 rarely mentions the strike, and within this period the strike in his telling is not yet clarified, still in ambiguous relation to intimidation, machine-breaking, and other nonstrike activities—the destined set of elisions that characterize the era. These facts tell us as much about the era's self-identifications as they do about its historians. Rudé's famous survey of 1730–1848 has under the entry *Strike* a redirection: "See labor disputes, Luddism, London, Paris."[2] No doubt these are all things one should see. The force of the substitution is to suggest that we should locate the strike as a delayed development within the larger genre of the labor dispute, a development that, as of 1848, had not yet appeared.

It would be foolish to dispute such a conclusion. Certainly that is the position presented persuasively by Shorter and Tilly:

---

1 Eric Hobsbawm, *The Age of Revolution: Europe 178–1848*, London: Abacus, 2007, 255, 141.

2 George Rudé, *The Crowd in History: A Study of Popular Disturbances in France and England, 1730–1848*, London: Lawrence and Wishart, 1984, 278.

In concentrating on the strike, we exclude a number of the other forms of conflict and of collective action (the two are by no means synonymous) ... That is convenient, since the strike is one of the easier forms of action to identify, trace and describe. The other forms of conflict, protest and self-expression which one might plausibly use to get some sense of changing orientations of workers include machine-breaking, sabotage, brawling, demonstrating, pamphlet-writing, perhaps turnover and absenteeism as well; all of them are much harder to pin down than strikes. The other forms of collective action workers have employed to accomplish common ends include the organization of political parties, mutual aid societies, conspiratorial groups, labor unions, insurance plans and many other cooperative ventures.[3]

The preservation of collective action's many modes, of the creativity of antagonism, is a vital task. But there are difficulties here as well, qualitative puzzles arising beyond the realm of quantitative scholarship. A first suggestion of the difficulty is the tendency to locate the strike's appearance at the inflection point where it becomes the lead tactic, rather than at the moment of its entrance into the theater of struggle. This has the effect of intimating an overly clear historical break between riot and strike. Moreover, the generic account in which strike comes into being as something like a condensation of the labor dispute conceals, surely against the intentions of our most deft historians, the strike's emergence from the riot, from circulation struggles. Rather than being complementary and genealogically conjoined, the two tactics are rigidly demarcated both in their nature and in their history, and set in opposition. This will later prove to be a problem for those trying to understand the riot's return.

---

3   Shorter and Tilly, *Strikes in France*, 4.

Spectacle and Discipline

The opposition of riot and strike is an avowed project of the nineteenth century persisting in various quarters thereafter. The binary is produced successfully some time around midcentury. Consider the distance between the Bull Ring Riots of 1839 and the Flint Glassmaker's Strike two decades later. Each ought to be recognized as exemplary of its genre. The former began with a series of political meetings held in Birmingham's Bull Ring market district. On July 4, the mayor and magistrates arrived and read the Riot Act, at which point police summoned from London set upon the crowd in ways that would draw broad and inevitable comparisons to Peterloo. Accordingly, a riot ensued. "Windows were smashed by bricks and hard lumps of sugar looted from Bourne's grocery before it was torched, and shuttered windows were attacked with iron bars torn from the fence," leaving wreckage enough that "the Duke of Wellington went so far as to compare Birmingham to cities he had seen sacked on the continent during his military campaigns."[4] More riots followed, in Birmingham and elsewhere.

In parallel with the rise of glass architecture, window-breaking came in the nineteenth century to define what Ian Hayward calls the "spectacular riot." In a canny comparison, Isobel Armstrong sets the 1839 riots against the successful strike of the Flint Glassmakers, begun in factories across several cities in December 1858 and extending into the new year. The strike, greatly debated both within the trade union and without, defines itself precisely against the riotous habits of 1839 et al. This is no wonder, given its constituency: "The practice of glass-breaking had no hold

---

4   Michael Weaver, "The Birmingham Bull Ring Riots of 1839: Variations on a Theme of Class Conflict," *Social Science Quarterly* 78: 1, March 1997, 146, 137.

on the glassworkers and their disciplined strike."[5] In this, its self-conception is paradigmatic of the modern labor action. The strike is exactly what the riot is not.

There can be little dispute that these two events are rightly named. The earlier is not the *echt*-form of the food riot, by then decades past its peak and decline. But it is close enough—not least for its launch from the marketplace, looting including seizure of foodstuffs, bloody battles with the state, and so on. The later action follows the format of strike in every regard. There is no mystery why it should wish so insistently to distinguish itself from the riot, given its need to make claims of legitimacy both against state repression and for support from other trade unions. By this juncture, the clear demarcation between—and indeed the contraposition of—strike and riot has *become* true.

This might be understood as the *ideology of collective action* cemented in the period, in which riot and strike take on a political opposition and even antagonism. The argument here is that this opposition is possible precisely because the two actions have been defined entirely according to their forms of appearance, which are taken to provide clear knowledge of their politics, their social content. Walter Benjamin remarks, "It is the peculiarity of *technological* forms of production (as opposed to art forms) that their progress and their success are proportionate to the *transparency* of their social content. (Hence glass architecture.)"[6] Industrial production, progress, glass

---

5 Isobel Armstrong, *Victorian Glassworlds: Glass Culture and the Imagination 1830–1880*, Oxford: Oxford University Press, 2008, 69. Armstrong also connects the two events via the odd eventuality that one of the Birmingham magistrates of 1839, William Chance, was a partner in one of England's great glassmaking firms.

6 Walter Benjamin, *The Arcades Project*, trans. Howard Eiland and Kevin McLaughlin, Cambridge, Mass.: Harvard University Press, 2002, 465 (emphasis in original).

architecture. This is the world of the strike. The ideology of collective action holds to this idea of transparency— that by peering at the surface one can see directly to the depths, have immediate access to social content. The strike becomes the strike via being *formalized* against the riot. It is order itself, the unbroken window. The riot, now defined equally as the strike's opposite number, must equally find its content in its form. But this has paradoxical consequences. Its form is disordered; disorder becomes its content. No one knows what the riot wants. It wants nothing but its own disorder, its bright opacity. Glints and shards of shattered glass.

The purpose is not to suggest that beneath this ideology there is a contrary truth; this is not how ideology works. We ought not suggest that riot and strike are one, or even close. The division of riot and strike is necessary and even obvious, and built on the most material changes in the political economy of the era. Rather, the hope is to be attentive to the risks of what might be lost by setting them in rigid and static opposition. In losing the history whereby strike emerges from riot, we lose the process of transformation itself and are left instead with its resultants standing before us as givens. This presents limits for adequate periodization within the history of capital. "Capitalism" is not a homogenous thing. Neither is it a politely serial phenomenon, one synchronic situation following discretely on another. Fredric Jameson, in his epochal literary methodology, insists (at a different scale), "What is synchronic is the 'concept' of the mode of production; the moment of the historical coexistence of several modes of production is not synchronic in this sense, but open to history in a dialectical way."[7] It is precisely the synchronization—riot's

---

7 Fredric Jameson, *The Political Unconscious: Narrative as Socially Symbolic Act*, Ithaca: Cornell University, 2014, 95.

with one phase of capital's development, strike's with another, a break between them—that obscures this situation. If our dating suggests that the era of riot ends before that of strike begins, this cannot offer full testimony on the shifting balance within capital itself, the changes ongoingly wrought by value's self-undermining dynamic.

Armstrong strains to overcome this limit, to leap across the dead space opened between riot and strike. From earlier riots she educes what she calls "the three cardinal principles of the grammar of glass-breaking—collective action, the body as property, and the refusal of abstraction"; these she finds reemergent in the later strike.[8] This is a subtle reading and insightful about crucial matters, not least the rejection of what she calls the patrician window-breaking code, in which "window-breaking is a nonformal act of violence, a certain *style* of crime without a content."[9]

And yet Armstrong's grammar retains a certain formalism, a certain discursive focus—as does Hayward's idea of the spectacular riot, which in the first instance might be grasped as a riposte to the new spectacle of urban, industrial modernity. The social content of both riot and strike cannot be limited to the principles of the participants, their affects and beliefs. What then is the strike's social content? It is twofold. As noted, it is labor's confrontation with capital in an attempt to set the price of labor power (against the zero price of unemployment). But the social content of the strike is also *productivity itself,* and this is all-important. It is not "capitalism" in some abstract or general sense from which the strike depends. Neither can it be reduced to the particular miseries of industrialism's machine-life, though nobody could doubt that these are a brutal spur. It is rather the set of changes attendant on the

---

8 Armstrong, *Victorian Glassworlds,* 73.

9 Ibid., 65 (emphasis in original).

traverse from commercial to industrial capital that drive the many toward the newly productive sectors and that drive capital to concentrate itself there as well—just as the many were previously driven into the market for subsistence in an uneven global process.

An evident if often neglected fact is that the limited, demand-based strike's effectiveness by and large coincides not with capital's frailty but with its vitality, when the wage-commodity circuit is yielding surplus value and accumulation. When production is not expanding, a capitalist has less interest in preserving its continuity and may endeavor to outlast strikers. "But to argue that an employer *could* outlast his striking workers," notes John Rule about early English strikes, "is not to say that it was always in his interest to do so. He would not want to forgo the high profits available from expanding output on a rising market. In such conditions it was more rational to concede than resist demands."[10]

Too Much and Too Little

Thus the category of production struggles, for which strike is archetype. The strike is the form of collective action proper to the productive phase of capital. It comes into being before that, tests itself against the world, but is able to realize itself only with capital's period of accumulation. This phase does not arrive punctually or autonomously when commercial or circulation-centered capital has exhausted itself, but rather emerges from and remains entwined with it. Production and circulation stand in a classically dialectical relation: both opposed and mutually constitutive, their

---

10   John Rule, *The Labouring Classes in Early Industrial England 1750–1850*, London: Addison Wesley Longman, 1986, 261 (emphasis in original).

contradiction (the contradiction between value and price) holding them in conjoined motion. The strike's source is the transformation that moves bodies and capital into the sphere of production. Not all of them, not all of it, we will continue to insist. But past a certain threshold. The strike emerges from circulation, but it becomes the leading tactic when the threshold is passed, when a quantitative change in the structure of the economy becomes qualitative. In the end, matters might be formulated thus: The strike ascends when the site of proletarian reproduction moves to the wage, which must at the same time become the crux of capital's own circuit of reproduction.

The purification and autonomization of the strike in the nineteenth century is therefore one-sided; it holds only the opposition of production and circulation, without their unity. That is to say, in the dialectic of continuity and break, the setting of strike against riot is necessary but insufficient, tilting too far toward a break, toward discontinuity and formal opposition. It will be important to recognize the moments when that continuity, now hidden behind the veil of historical change, becomes visible.

We might return to 1839 simply to recover the heterogeneity of the moment. The political meetings that inspire the violence are Chartist gatherings, naturally. Standardbearers of Shelley's many, they are the most advanced labor organization in Britain. Their paper, *The North Star*, prints "To The People"—the passage from "Masque of Anarchy" including the famous verse—in April 1839. In May it prints a poem by "E.H. (A Factory Girl of Stalybridge)," and in June an anonymous poem, "Lines by a Factory Operative." This is the current issue when the Bull Ring Riots begin.[11]

---

11 Mike Sanders, *The Poetry of Chartism: Aesthetic, Politics, History*, Cambridge: Cambridge University Press, 2009, 233.

The organized labor movement is already well along. As Eric Hobsbawm has it,

> In Britain the attempts to link all laboring men together in "general trades' unions," i.e., to break through the sectional and local isolation of particular groups of workers to the national, perhaps even the universal solidarity of the laboring class, began in 1818 and were pursued with feverish intensity between 1829 and 1834.[12]

So it is not so easy to get a fix on the politics of the Bull Ring. This uncertainty will pale against the events of three years later, perhaps the most undecidable in Great Britain's nineteenth century. The mystery is all there in a single sentence: "The point of spontaneous social combustion in Britain was reached in the unplanned Chartist general strike of the summer of 1842 (the so-called 'plug riots')."[13]

"Spontaneous," "unplanned." We will want to mark these words; we know all too well they mean the riot. The episode leaps from the Staffordshire miners to factories, mills, and mines across Great Britain, finally gathering more than a million workers into its sweep. It bears the basic features of the labor strike rather perfectly: It takes the form of work refusal. Following on three years of industrial breakdown, its main demands, passed as resolutions throughout the action, concern the length of the working day and the restoration of wages to 1820 levels, as well as rent reductions. Hobsbawm continues to insist, however, that it is both too much strike and too little: "The general strike proved inapplicable under Chartism, except (in 1842) as a spontaneously spreading hunger-riot."[14] In

---

12   Hobsbawm, *Age of Revolution*, 255.
13   Ibid., 208.
14   Ibid., 256–7.

all of this, he seems anxious to recognize that the strike and riot might be continuous while still trying to preserve an idea of the pure strike as something else again. It's a muddle. But that muddle is the truth of things.

These slippages are the inevitable outcome of letting form stand too easily for content. They are also signs of Jameson's coexistence, of the presence of tensions within the diachronic spiral of capital. As such, they make other moments of coexistence, other moments of metamorphosis within capital and thus in its forms of collective action, thinkable. Since the weight of this book tilts toward thinking a complementary metamorphosis in the present, this is suggestive indeed.

CHAPTER 5

The General Strike

This ideology of collective action, with its static opposition of riot and strike, would in turn be elided with a corresponding opposition at a higher conceptual stratum, that of anarchism and socialism. It may appear from within the conventions of the present that specific tactics and accompanying repertoires arise from, and are thus proper to, particular political and analytical positions.[1] Historically, the ideological opposition of tactics has helped produce the political opposition, and this would in turn consolidate further the antithesis of forms of action.

In the present day the strike, and with it the broader category of organized labor actions and large-scale organization as such, is understood as the political-economic tactic associated with the complex field of socialism and communism as political horizons, conjoining with historical materialist thought. The riot, and with it the collection of "insurrectionary" tactics before and beyond traditional labor organization, is understood in opposition to this. It is a spontaneous attack on daily life, but also the rejection of a purportedly deterministic, authoritarian, and implicitly if not explicitly statist political program. One of this book's basic questions concerns whether this set of indexed oppositions, a formula with real historical reason, still makes sense.

---

1   Marxism being not a political belief (much less a program), but rather a mode of analysis.

The split in the First International surely needs no rehearsal here, and a full unfolding of the divergence between anarchists on the one hand and on the other socialists and communists is beyond the scope of this study.[2] It is worth recalling the extent to which these positions were at first far more continuous than they now appear; in parallel with that of riot and strike, their polarization is a historical procedure. At the time of the First International, the rhetoric of the emancipation of labor as a fundamental project was shared, along with the centrality of the proletariat and the presupposition of class war as basis for revolution. Debates of the era are illustrative. One might consider the dispute between collectivist anarchism and anarchist communism in the 1870s. The former fraction wished to do away with all market exchange and wages, while in the vision of the latter, "an exchange economy still operates within a network of worker-owned, self-managed 'collectivities' that hold legal ownership of the instruments and resources of production." Wage labor and its status took on decisive importance. Kristin Ross writes, "Additionally—and this was the point of greatest fracture between the two groups—collectivist anarchism retained the wage system by making the distinction of food and other goods dependent on the labor contribution each individual made."[3]

---

2   It is a kind of question-begging to distinguish between socialism and communism. The intent, which will be relevant later, is much the same as that in Moishe Postone's term "traditional Marxism," which we take to be socialism—referring to a political horizon of socializing the means of production under worker control via seizure of the state, whereas "communism" refers to the political horizon of abolishing the mode of production altogether. On the question of whether the former can lead to the latter, as proposed in Marx's *Critique of the Gotha Program*, some brief thoughts are offered in the final chapter.

3   Kristin Ross, *Communal Luxury: The Political Imaginary of the Paris Commune*, London: Verso, 2015, 107.

Such positions and debates regarding the contents of a revolutionary society make clear that the rigid antithesis of the political positions descending from the split would be fashioned over time. The mapping of tactics onto political and analytical positions does not simply happen along the way, but rather is part of this fashioning. Nowhere is the process staged more explicitly than in the case of the general strike. The debates concerning the general strike present difficulties not least for various distinctions drawn (and not drawn) between "proletarian" and "political" general strikes, between the "general" and the "mass" strike. Fortunately for us, parsing these distinctions is less what is at stake than is one particular moment within the debates and the possibilities it puts on offer for considering the relation of tactics to political positions.

The victory within the International of the socialist position regarding models of political struggle had already been ratified in advance of the 1872 scission. Resolution No. 9 from the previous year affirmed, "this constitution of the working class into a political party is indispensable in order to ensure the triumph of the social revolution and its ultimate end—the abolition of classes." The commitment to a parliamentary process implies both a certain kind of organization and at least some observance of a legalistic standard. The parliamentary strategy will come and go, but the organizational logic of the party, which accompanies it, will achieve greater constancy. As an expression of its organizational basis, supposedly orderly in its execution, and entering into confrontation with capital rather than the state, the narrow strike cannot help but adhere to such a political horizon, even as any given strike will likely have more local ambitions.

Against this, the seeming disorder of anarchist modes of struggle becomes an object of antipathy. *Spontaneity* is the keyword encoding this antipathy. It is an ambiguous term, politically. Often it indicates an action arising "naturally," a momentary response. In this sense a spontaneous act is slave to stimulus. However, according to another definition, "in the eighteenth century, when Kant described the transcendental unity of apperception—the fact that I am aware of myself as having my own experiences—he called this a spontaneous act. Kant meant the opposite of something natural. A spontaneous act is one that is freely undertaken."[4] Thus the term preserves both the sense of autonomic upwelling (recalling the spasmodic view of the riot) and that of the willed act, freely chosen, which nonetheless lacks the patient development of counterorganization moving in parallel with capital's developments.

The term takes on an even more vexed complexity with the Soviet revolution. Lenin will famously wield it to deplore disorganized masses. The Russian word, *stikhiinost,* signifies both spontaneity and the chaos of nature: that which has the least degree of organization. Alexander Bogdanov, a Russian polymath philosopher, will specify that this disorder of nature is a resistance to that organization which is human labor, and that the two stand in opposition: "Consequently, the world is a battlefield of collective labor, in which human activity struggles with the spontaneous resistance of nature."[5]

It is the unstated collapse of these senses—chaotic, natural, contra human labor—that enables the term to take on its most pejorative dimensions. From a Leninist orthodoxy, spontaneism becomes not simply lack of organization

---

4   "Spontaneity, Mediation, Rupture," *Endnotes* 3, 2013, 232. The collective authors cite Robert Pippin, *Hegel's Idealism*, Cambridge: Cambridge University Press, 1989, 16–24.

5   Maria Chehonadskih, "The Anthropocene in 90 Minutes," mute.com.

in some sense, but also antagonism to labor, and thus implicitly to the proletariat. Moreover, a disagreement with organizational strategies can be transcoded as unreason, contrary not just to labor but also to the human as such.

In an earlier moment of this debate staged in light of the Paris Commune, Marx at first argues gravely against such an approach, against impatient revolutionizing. Amid the crushing French defeats of 1870, he cautions, "The French workmen ... must not allow themselves to be swayed by the national *souvenirs* of 1792 ..." Instead, they must "build up the future. Let them calmly and resolutely improve the opportunities of republican liberty, for the work of their own class organization."[6] As is well known, he will later change his position and render an entirely remarkable verdict on the Commune.

Engels and Sorel

Marx's initial doubts return in Engels's assessment of the general strike hazarded by the Bakuninists in 1873, with Spain on the brink of civil war. Engels's conclusions surely haunt Hobsbawm's later vacillation, his identification of general strike with riot—two avatars of excessive spontaneity and inadequate organization, the identity of too much and too little. "The general strike, in the Bakuninists' program, is the lever which will be used for introducing the social revolution," he writes, dialing up the coruscating scorn. He continues:

> One fine morning all the workers in every industry in a country, or perhaps in every country, will cease work, and thereby compel the ruling class either to submit in about

---

6   Karl Marx and V. I. Lenin, *The Civil War in France: The Paris Commune*, New York: International Publishers, 1968, 34.

four weeks, or to launch an attack on the workers so that the latter will have the right to defend themselves, and may use the opportunity to overthrow the old society.

Reaching back to 1842 and its limitations, its failures of coordination and preparation, he then comes to "the crux of the question":

> On the one hand, the governments, especially if they are encouraged by the workers' abstention from political action, will never allow the funds of the workers to become large enough, and on the other hand, political events and the encroachments of the ruling class will bring about the liberation of the workers long before the proletariat gets the length of forming this ideal organization and this colossal reserve fund. But if they had these, they would not need to make use of the roundabout way of the general strike in order to attain their object.[7]

The anarchists, in this telling, lack both reason and resource. Having not developed their labor associations adequately, the workers will have accrued neither adequate organizational capacity nor sufficient finances to stage what they believe to be a battle for total emancipation. Rosa Luxemburg finds in this what will become the commonsense of social democracy, derived from its other, the "anarchist theory of the general strike—that is, the theory of the general strike as a means of inaugurating the social revolution, in contradistinction to the daily political struggle of the working class." Any defense of the

---

7 Friedrich Engels, "The Bakuninists at Work: An Account of the Spanish Revolt in the Summer of 1873," cited in Rosa Luxemburg, *The Essential Rosa Luxemburg*, ed. Helen Scott, Chicago: Haymarket Books, 2008, 111–12.

anarchist general strike "exhausts itself in the following simple dilemma: either the proletariat as a whole are not yet in possession of the powerful organization and financial resources required, in which case they cannot carry through the general strike, or they are sufficiently well organized, in which case they do not need the general strike."[8]

Georges Sorel will offer a remarkable defense nonetheless. Before passing to this, we might note in Engels an interesting assumption about the development of a strike fund, the heavy artillery in the arsenal of the proletariat. The limit to its expansion is the state, which "will never allow the funds of the workers to become large enough." This is the world seen from the perspective of accumulation, wherein a growing social surplus is assumed, and the contest to appropriate the greatest share possible of that surplus is the plausible and necessary preamble to enlarged struggle. Engels's conception of the grounds for struggle is productivist, not only in the abstract sense of assuming the centrality of productive labor to revolutionary struggle, but also in its presupposition of a concrete and ongoing increase in social wealth arising from productive capital; it dovetails with Rule's remark about the successful strike's dependence on "expanding output." This is the unmarked historical particularity from which Engels universalizes his criticism.

Sorel will be Engels's opposite number more than thirty years on. His defense of the general strike is no less ardent than Engels's denunciation of it, while sharing that denunciation's universalizing tendency. For Sorel, the power of the general strike is not its capacity to bring capital into instant submission, but its provision to the proletarian of a total orientation, a political totalization.

---

8 Luxemburg, *Essential*, 112.

He distinguishes between a "proletarian" and "political" general strike. The latter is understood as a mechanism called by political actors in control of centralized unions with the goal of transferring power from one government to another already prepared and organized. This is the "ideal organization" that Engels finds impossible. Sorel's gesture is not to insist contra Engels on the possibility of this organization. Instead he rejects it for preserving political domination, for its projection onto the general strike this "political" character in which the horizon is the seizure of state power and centralized state control. The proletarian general strike, conversely, is the precondition for emancipatory class war.

Here Sorel sets the proletarian general strike against the limited or narrow strike, suggesting that the latter offers partial satisfactions and gains that serve to dim revolutionary fervor. Further, it reveals but does not resolve the differing interests between common workers and the labor aristocracy of "foremen, clerks, engineers, etc.," as well as the seemingly opposed interests of the peasantry and industrial proletariat. Marx's sense of capital as a totality and his abstraction of social existence into two antagonistic classes cannot be grasped from this perspective, nor can it be built up piecemeal.

The general strike unifies the experience of quotidian miseries and the fragmentary glimpses of something beyond them, allowing the individual worker an intuition of the world toward which revolution strives, obtained "as a whole, perceived instantaneously."[9] This Bergsonian "total knowledge" at the same time overcomes the practical problem of class disunity. Sorel imagines resolving the so-called composition problem in this way: "But all

---

9   Georges Sorel, *Reflections on Violence*, ed. Jeremy Jennings, Cambridge: Cambridge University Press, 1999, 128. See footnote 17 on that page regarding Bergson.

oppositions become extraordinarily clear when conflicts are supposed to be enlarged to the size of the general strike … society is plainly divided into two camps, and only into two, on a field of battle."[10]

Spontaneous action, therefore, is corollary to spontaneous knowledge in Kant's sense. This provides the only possible passage to actualized class consciousness and revolutionary possibility that is not trapped in advance by reified organizational structures: *the general strike must be taken as a whole and undivided, and the passage from capitalism to Socialism conceived as a catastrophe, the development of which baffles description."*[11] Though Sorel was a heretic socialist and syndicalist, it is this counter-position to state and party organization that becomes the familiar anarchist position on the general strike.

The Inversion of Rosa Luxemburg

Luxemburg's reconstruction of this question in "The Mass Strike" stands as one of the great political pamphlets on record, as much for its method as for its conclusion. It is not without its ambiguities. Here she seems to distinguish general and mass strike as phenomena of the nineteenth and twentieth centuries respectively, there to treat them as the same: "anarchism, with which the idea of the mass strike is indissolubly associated." She concedes that Engels's criticism of this strike "is at first glance so simple and so irrefutable that, for a quarter of a century, it has rendered excellent service to the modern labor movement against the anarchist phantom and as a means of carrying out the idea of political struggle to the largest circle of workers."[12]

---

10 Sorel, *Reflections*, 132.
11 Ibid., 148 (emphasis in original).
12 Luxemburg, *Essential*, 114, 112.

Her rhetoric here is supple and leading, potentially mis-leading. It suggests that any refutation of Engels's verdict must thus take the side of the "anarchist phantom." This has proved a durable misreading of Luxemburg, whose position is often adduced to a Sorelian spontaneity. "Rosa Luxemburg laid great emphasis on the spontaneity of the masses," begins one summary of received wisdom; it cites representative remarks to the effect that Luxemburg had "a fanatical but utopian, almost anarchist, faith in the masses."[13] Sorel himself reports that the "*new school* which calls itself Marxist, Syndicalist, and revolutionary"—he means Luxemburg, perhaps Anton Pannekoek—"declared in favor of the general strike as soon as it became clearly conscious of the true sense of its own doctrine."[14]

But for Luxemburg it is not doctrinal consciousness that has changed. It is material circumstances. One cannot blame Engels for his reasoning in 1873; it is those who remain trapped in that position against new historical developments who are worthy of scorn. Pannekoek will make a similar argument shortly thereafter. In the face of Kautsky's polemic against the mass strike, which Kautsky feared would harm the Social Democratic Party and its trade unions, Pannekoek holds that "various forms of action ... are not polar opposites, but part of a gradually differentiated range," forms taking their shifting salience from the development of economic forces.[15]

Luxemburg writes her pamphlet in train of a series of expanding mass strikes, first in Belgium and Sweden, then

---

13   Norman Geras, *The Legacy of Rosa Luxemburg,* London: Verso, 1976, 111–12. Second passage cites E. H. Carr.

14   Sorel, *Reflections,* 120.

15   Anton Pannekoek, *Pannekoek and Gorter's Marxism,* ed. D. A. Smart, London: Pluto, 1978, 65. In retrospect, how easy it was to down Kautsky in debate!

the Netherlands, Russia and Italy; then the insurrectionary wave of strikes that constitute the incomplete Russian
Revolution of 1905. She confronts the strike thus not as
error but eventuality:

> If, therefore, the Russian Revolution teaches us anything,
> it teaches above all that the mass strike is not artificially
> "made," not "decided" at random, not "propagated,"
> but that it is a historical phenomenon which, at a given
> moment, results from social conditions with historical inev-
> itability. It is not, therefore, by abstract speculations on the
> possibility or impossibility, the utility or the injuriousness
> of the mass strike, but only by an examination of those
> factors and social conditions out of which the mass strike
> grows in the present phase of the class struggle—in other
> words, it is not by *subjective criticism* of the mass strike
> from the standpoint of what is desirable, but only by *objec-
> tive investigation* of the sources of the mass strike from
> the standpoint of what is historically inevitable, that the
> problem can be grasped or even discussed.[16]

Her investigation reveals a profoundly complex situation
in Russia. She describes the lead-up to the January mass
strike in St. Petersburg:

> Here was the eight-hour day fought for, there piece-work
> was resisted, here were brutal foremen "driven off" in a
> sack on a handcar, at another place infamous systems of
> fines were fought against, everywhere better wages were
> striven for and here and there the abolition of homework.[17]

---

16   Luxemburg, *Essential*, 117–8 (emphasis in original).
17   Ibid., 129.

In this circumstance of manifold grievances, no political coordination from above is possible. However, the internal spread of the strike within the proletariat becomes possible. What renders a consistency to these various Russian particulars is the transition from a quasi-feudal absolutism toward an industrializing capital. While urban labor and the peasantry may find themselves in quite different positions, both positions float within this singular transformation, and the relay between loosely political and economic struggles is open, challenging the separation that Anthony Giddens calls a fundamental basis of the capitalist state.[18] Thus a shift in balance, from the front of absolutism to that of economic struggles that follow the January strike, becomes possible. This for Luxemburg opens onto a revolutionary prospect:

> But at the same time, the period of the economic struggles of the spring and summer of 1905 made it possible for the urban proletariat, by means of active social democratic agitation and direction, to assimilate later all the lessons of the January prologue and to grasp clearly all the further tasks of the revolution.[19]

Spontaneity, then, can unfold into coordination in given conditions, those of transition. This is the revolutionary sequence Luxemburg sees before her, and the mass strike is the form this sequence takes. This does not, for her, validate the anarchist position. Her conclusion, offered at the outset, is in fact brutal in this regard. The revolutionary character and success of the mass strike "not merely does not afford a vindication of anarchism, but actually

---

18 Anthony Giddens, *The Class Structure of the Advanced Societies*, London: Hutchinson, 1973, 206.

19 Luxemburg, *Essential*, 131.

means *the historical liquidation of anarchism.*"[20] Because of political-economic developments, the mass strike has, as it were, changed sides; in an objective movement, it has entered the repertoire of communist struggle.

One might now read Luxemburg as a blow struck for socialism and Marxism against anarchist imaginings. In moments, the pamphlet takes on such triumphalist tonalities, not to its credit. One might read it as a recommendation of how to proceed, of the importance of the mass strike weapon; no doubt this is central.

It may be most significant to the present, however, to read the tract for its dialectical clarity. When material conditions change, when the political-economic structure changes, the political import and practical possibilities of a tactic of collective action might change as well. The frozen association of strike and accompanying forms of political organization with what we will now move to calling communist theory should be abandoned. Just so the frozen association of supposedly spontaneous collective action with anarchism. The thinkers who hold to these identifications, for all their intellectual cunning or principled rejection of theoretical trends, can only be our Kautskys, or for that matter Bömelburgs, trapped in the amber of "what is desirable." We must be open to "a fundamental revision of the old standpoint of Marxism," one based in the transformations of social reality.[21] One does not declare that a communist does this or an anarchist does that. One goes to "the standpoint of what is historically inevitable"—from that standpoint alone "the problem can be grasped or even discussed."

---

20   Ibid., 113 (emphasis in original).
21   Ibid., 114.

CHAPTER 6

Crossed Wires, Or, Strike to Riot

In 1963, the socialist journal *Monthly Review* gave over the breadth of a double issue to a Detroit auto worker: an accurate descriptor underscoring the common quality of James Boggs's trajectory, inextricable from his remarkable life. In 1937, following the path of the first Great Migration of black Americans from the rural South to the industrial North and Midwest, Boggs had moved from Alabama to Detroit, where he would live the rest of his life. He would eventually marry Grace Lee, the third leader and theorist of the Johnson-Forrest Tendency along with C. L. R. James and Raya Dunayevskaya. The tendency originated within the Workers' Party and the Socialist Workers' Party, two Trotskyist groups; it preserved a workerist perspective and had given particular attention to militant wildcat strikes among miners and autoworkers.

Given this cluster of circumstances, affiliations, and commitments, Boggs's brief foreword to his *The American Revolution: Pages From a Negro Worker's Notebook* is startling. It concludes,

> I am a factory worker but I know more than just factory work. I know the difference between what would sound right if one lived in a society of logical people and what is right when you live in a society of real people with real differences. It may sound perfectly natural to a highly

educated and logical person, even when he hears people saying that there is going to be a big riot, to assume that there will not be a big riot because the authorities have everything under control. But if I kept hearing people say that there was going to be a big riot and *I* saw one of these logical people standing in the middle, I would tell him he'd better get out of the way because he sure was going to get killed.

Reforms and revolutions are created by the illogical actions of people. Very few logical people ever make reforms and none make revolutions. Rights are what you make and what you take.[1]

It is a curious passage and not only for its closing gesture of what we might call *instrumental irrationality*. On the one hand it is a bit opaque; the sudden apparition of the riot is unmotivated to say the least, or disorientingly prescient. Nineteen sixty-three is four years before Detroit's Great Rebellion, at the time the largest-scale riot in national history. And it is a year before rebellions in Harlem and elsewhere will inaugurate the period in which the "race riot" ascends as a central feature of the U.S.' political landscape.

On the other hand, the reasoning that moves through the passage is familiar, if one has spent a few moments with the implicit debate's history. It tacitly associates labor organizing with "logic," with a kind of orderliness that can't but mirror the congealed rationality of the factory assembly line. The riot goes with disorder, illogic, the ambient social space of rumor. No less significantly, the passage recovers Luxemburg's overcoming of prescriptive politics. Its distinction between "what *would* sound right if one lived in a society of logical people" and "the real"

---

1   James Boggs, *Pages from a Black Radical's Notebook: A James Boggs Reader*, Detroit: Wayne State University Press, 2011, 84–5.

of what actually happens within given social conditions is a version of Luxemburg's opposition of the politically "desirable" and "historically inevitable."

Each of them find the particularity of their moment, of its openness, uncertainty, possibility. The sixties give rise to a unique situation of riot and strike, one that is at its most concentrated in Detroit. The situation there has two distinct features. One is the racialization of the riot, or rather, the relationship between riot and racialization. That is the theme of a later chapter. The other, which can scarcely be disarticulated from the matter of race, is the sheer nearness of the two forms of collective action—their coexistence, adjacency, confrontation. This is a revelatory puzzle of the decade, an entanglement that as it develops and clarifies begins to disclose how the riot will not only express but explicate its historical moment.

The most revealing and predictive associations of riot and strike are those with given political-economic conditions that orient capital as a whole and change over time, allowing the forms of action to change in their meaning and their power. This indexing is not absolute; political-economic conditions are not absolutely determining. Rather they suggest both possibilities and limits. The field of social contest is held in tension by, on the one hand, the capacity of humans to "make their own history," and on the other, "circumstances existing already, given and transmitted from the past." It is because of the tension between these forces, between agency and determination, that we find multiple forms of collective action within a given conjuncture. At the same time, because a given set of conditions tilts one way and not another, one among the forms of action will tend to become the leading tactic.

In periods of systemic transformation, there will necessarily be shifts in the leading tactics, and competitions among tactics, as different fractions of society, differently positioned, assay emancipatory struggles. The sixties and seventies in the United States offer an extraordinary study of this phenomenon of transformation, equivalent to what we saw in the early nineteenth century in Great Britain— although here, the wind of change blows in the opposite direction, from the factory back toward the port, the market, the public square. For all the manifest differences, there are resonances of nineteenth-century machine-breaking, as tidal shifts in social production manifest themselves as undecidability and transformation within the repertoire of tactics. With the strike now a distinct and popular tactic, the return of the riot appears at first as a strange and heroic effort to *conjoin the two forms of action into a revolutionary process* in which the labor struggle and the riot seem two fronts of a single antagonism. "I am a factory worker but I know more than just factory work," says Boggs; it could be the decade speaking. The decade's ceaseless struggle and invention, largely centered among a black population bearing the early weight of deindustrialization, is possible only within a very narrow window. It is an effort pursued sidelong, desperately, perhaps behind the back of consciousness, and one ultimately unable to realize itself.

Struggle and Profit

The strike survives as leading tactic in the industrialized west through the sixties. Much as Engels intimated, it is yoked to economic expansion. Over the course of the twentieth century, the strike attends not economic catastrophe but growth, a fact no less true in the thirties of the Depression and the Popular Front than during the postwar boom, as noted by the sociologist Roberto Franzosi:

Quantitative research has shown beyond doubt, across different institutional settings (sample periods and countries) that strike frequency follows the business cycle and the movement of unemployment in particular—the higher the level of unemployment, the lower the level of strikes.[2]

For all the clarity of this correlation, the traditional strike's association with low unemployment is part of a larger dynamic of systemic accumulation and expanding industrialization inexorably linked to high profit rates. Accumulation, it must be remarked, is not a fluent and unvexed process even when viewed from a distance. The long metacycle of productive capital in the west from about 1830 to 1973 is rife with volatility, crises, recessions, and one transfer between hegemonic powers. Within this variegated historical landscape, nonetheless, the correlation between strikes, taut labor markets, industrial expansion, and high profit rates is overwhelming; the causality is logically necessary. It is premised on relative difficulties in replacing labor, capital's unwillingness to interrupt highly profitable activities, the state's ability to purchase the domestic peace with social wages, and labor's capacity to increase its position and its store insofar as there is social surplus to be appropriated.

The sixties in this regard are an unusual period. Profit rates remain historically high. World real GDP growth for the decade is over 5 percent, more than a full percentage point above the preceding and following decades, driven by the Anglosphere and northern Europe, with Japan growing even more swiftly in its accelerated catch-up.

---

2   Roberto Franzosi, "One Hundred Years of Strike Statistics: Data, Methodology, and Theoretical Issues in Quantitative Strike Research," CRSO Working Paper No. 257, Ann Arbor: Center for Research on Social Organization, 1982, 15, 17.

Manufacturing net profit rates in the U.S. have peaks equal to, and averages higher than, any other period of the boom.[3] Consequently, the "withering away of the strike" across northern Europe, the U.K., the U.S., and Canada foreseen by some economists—wagering that within "mature labor movement ... members are not so predisposed toward strikes as they formerly were"—did not come to pass.[4]

At the same time macroeconomic weakness begins to appear, expansion slowing as the pooling profits seek, increasingly in vain, for a productive outlet, initiating "the signal crisis of the U.S. regime of accumulation of the late 1960s and early 1970s."[5] Corresponding attempts to increase purchasing power lead not to renewed production but to inflation and capital flight, in the lurch toward the crisis of 1973 that would signal the decline of the U.S.-led cycle of accumulation. Brenner tracks the decline of the U.S. industrial sector, and of manufacturing more broadly, in the face of international competition, a phenomenon of which the automakers are, as ever, leading examples. The effect of this decline, "especially given the enormous fraction of the total for the advanced capitalist economies represented by U.S. production—was a major fall in the aggregate profitability of the advanced capitalist economies, located primarily in manufacturing, in the years between 1965 and 1973."[6] That the global slowdown has its basis in a U.S. industrial engine suggests it may be possible to generalize, at least in limited ways, from the U.S. experience.

---

3   Robert Brenner, "What's Good for Goldman Sachs," prologue to *The Economics of Global Turbulence*, Madrid: Akal, 2009, page numbers taken from typescript provided by author, 8, 11.

4   Arthur M. Ross and Paul T. Hartman, *Changing Patterns of Industrial Conflict*, New York: Wiley, 1960, 71, 43.

5   Giovanni Arrighi, *The Long Twentieth Century*, 315.

6   Brenner, *Turbulence*, 38.

It is a paradoxical economy, with high productivity shadowed by incipient deindustrialization. Strikes persist: In the United Kingdom, the sixties would see a notable increase in both work stoppages and total working days lost. In the United States, the strike would experience an autumnal flare-up beginning around 1964 and lasting into the seventies—it could not be known that this would be the last golden gleam before winter came for the labor movement at the heart of the capitalist world system.[7] At the same time, there is a rapidly ascending visibility of riots on all scales, most famously in the series of "Long Hot Summers." The new era of riots has not yet arrived in earnest, but the uneven transition has begun.

In her study of the carceral state in California, Ruth Wilson Gilmore limns the way that a racialized population mobilizes between local oppressions and systematic collapse:

The 1965 Watts Rebellion was a conscious enactment of opposition (even if "spontaneous" in a Leninist sense) to inequality in Los Angeles, where everyday apartheid was forcibly renewed by police under the direction of the unabashedly white supremacist Chief William Parker. In Oakland, the Black Panther Party was conceived as a dramatic, highly disciplined, and easy-to-emulate challenge to local police brutality. Militant Black urban antiracist organizing that focused on attacking the concrete ways in which "race ... is the modality through which class is lived"

---

7 U.K. data from the Office for National Statistics, "Labour Disputes Annual Estimates; United Kingdom; 1891–2014" (version updated July 16, 2015), ons.gov.uk; US data from the Bureau of Labor Statistics, "Economic News Release: Table 1. Work stoppages involving 1,000 or more workers, 1947–2014" (version updated February 11, 2015), bls.gov.

emerged from many decades of struggle in the bloody crucible of revolution against *both* southern apartheid *and* its
doppelgänger in northern cities ...

In 1967 the system began to come apart symbolically
and materially. During the Summer of Love, as thousands
of flower children flocked to San Francisco to repudiate the
establishment, California lined up its *anti*-antiracist coer-
cive forces behind the vanguard Panther Gun Bill—all of
this at the same time that the rate of profit began its spectacular decline.[8]

Even the famously anodyne *Kerner Report*, commissioned
by Lyndon Johnson after the Newark riots and the Great
Rebellion in 1967, registers "a gradual shift in both tactics
and goals" within black protest "from legal to direct
action, from middle and upper class to mass action ... from
appealing to the sense of fair play of white Americans to
demands based upon the power of the black ghetto."[9]

The contours of the modern riot, *riot prime,* here begin
to stand clear. While sharing certain characteristics and
logics with older riots, it enters into a very different historical situation and confronts an alien landscape. It is crucial
therefore to note that the sequence *riot-strike-riot prime*
does not suggest a simple historical oscillation but a long
and arching development that both exhausts and retrieves
forms as the contents and contexts of struggle change.
Because this trajectory traces broader social changes
that occur in different degrees across the overdeveloped
world, certain kinships can be observed despite national or

---

8   Ruth Wilson Gilmore, *Golden Gulag: Prisons, Surplus, Crisis,
and Opposition in Globalizing California*, Berkeley and Los Angeles:
University of California Press, 2007, 39–40 (emphases in original).

9   Otto Kerner et al., *Report of the National Advisory Commission on Civil Disorders*, New York: Bantam, 1968, 227.

regional differences, for example among riots in the United Kingdom and France.

Riot prime in the United States is a new phase of racialized struggle emerging from and against the history of the more reform-oriented Civil Rights movement that by 1965 has largely won the victories it will win. The new riot's racialization stands out even more clearly against the backdrop of organized labor, not least for this backdrop's coded whiteness. Routinely precipitated by the violence of state actors and their ensuing impunity, *riot prime* must be thought of not only in the context of racial state violence but also, for example, in that of the aggressive racism of the AFL craft unions, which succeeded in deferring the formation of any black-led unions until the 1925 charter of the Brotherhood of Sleeping Car Porters. That is to say, the blackness of the riot appears not just as a vexed continuity with the Civil Rights movement against the antiblackness of the state but also against the whiteness of the strike. This comes to structure common sense itself—despite the long history of contrary examples on either side of the supposed binary, from the white-on-white "nativist" riots in the nineteenth century and the wave of anti-Asian attacks following the Chinese Exclusion Act down to the Delano Grape Growers Strike.

There is an evident paradox. On the one hand, the subject of the contemporary riot in the west is consistently racialized, and longstanding patterns of racialized violence, containment, and abjection are inseparable from the development of the modern riot. On the other, the absolute and eventually naturalized identification of tactic with race will turn out to be a destructive mistake, a confusion of correlation and cause—as if blackness itself were the origin of riot. Janet Abu-Lughod underscores the limits of the term "race riot," noting the constructedness of *race* and, further, the inadequacy of the term *riot* against the more openly political senses available to the language of uprising and rebellion. In the end she retains it "because it has an apparently clear reference in the literature to interracial violence, whether initiated by collectivities of whites against blacks or by collectivities of blacks against whites."[10] Significantly, the history of race riots in the United States begins with whites disciplining insubordinate other populations. The "Red Summer" of 1919, which would help forge profound but now largely forgotten bonds between U.S. blacks and socialist and communist organizations, is the best-known but scarcely the only example, itself bracketed within "an extraordinary wave of mass violence directed toward blacks between 1919 and 1923."[11] By the second half of the twentieth century, *race riot* summons images of spontaneous black violence. It is only then that the term comes to stand for riot as such. The rhetorical convergence is crude and effective. The purportedly thoughtless and natural character of riot, lacking reason, organization, and political mediation, is aligned with the racist tradition wherein racialized subjects are figured as natural, animalistic, irrational, immediate.

Revolutions Per Minute

In 1968, the Italian Socialist Party of Proletarian Unity deadlocked over an invitation to its international conference in 1968: a Black Panther or someone from the radical labor movement in Detroit? Their great good fortune was to discover that John Watson was a central member of both

---

10 Janet Abu-Lughod, *Race, Space, and Riots in Chicago, New York, and Los Angeles*, Oxford: Oxford University Press, 2007, 7, 11.

11 Michael C. Dawson, *Blacks In and Out of the Left*, Cambridge: Harvard University Press, 2013, 20.

the Dodge Revolutionary Union Movement (DRUM) and the leading Black Power group. This situation would not last. "Watson's membership in two separate revolutionary organizations, DRUM and the Panthers, represented a short-lived compromise between revolutionary forces in Detroit and California" which would collapse soon after.[12]

This moment is the crux of a mercurial political sequence. Even the most foreshortened recounting offers a sense of the rapid turnover of revolutionary formations. The prehistory must include the rise of U.S. industrialization in Detroit, as well as the founding there of the Nation of Islam, led by unemployed autoworker Elijah Muhammad. Between 1920 and 1970, Detroit's black population increases from 4 to 45 percent; this is the most dramatic locus of a broader internalization of black labor into the industrial proletariat, itself a motive force in the successes of Civil Rights movement and the fraying of formal Jim Crow.[13] The early sixties see the development of UHURU, an active chapter of the national Revolutionary Action Movement (RAM), and in 1966 the founding of the Detroit chapter of the Black Panther Party for Self-Defense. Then the Great Rebellion in the summer of 1967, featuring among other things a number of rooftop snipers warding off the police. In the autumn of Detroit's discontent, the *Inner City Voice*, a black militant newspaper led by Watson out of Wayne State University offices, becomes a nexus for various militant struggles; its staff includes figures central to all of the period's groupings. The next year, DRUM forms and then several other RUMs; in 1969 they conjoin as the League of Revolutionary Black Workers (LRBW). In 1970, the

---

12   Dan Georgakas and Marvin Surkin, *Detroit: I Do Mind Dying: A Study in Urban Revolution*, Chicago: Haymarket Books, 2012, 50.

13   Data available on the Detroit History webpage, "Population of Various Ethnic Groups," historydetroit.com.

Detroit chapter of the Panthers is shut down, perhaps on orders from the powerful Chicago chapter; well before this, "the ideological tensions between the Panthers and the League had become public knowledge."[14] In 1970 the LRBW begins an extended and painful scission, divided among tendencies supporting struggle on the cultural front, parliamentary engagement, formation of workers' councils, and a black vanguardist party. By 1972, the remainder of the LRBW affiliates with the Communist League and ceases to exist as an autonomous entity. Insofar as it is ever possible to make punctual claims, the sequence is over, and with it, the long sixties.[15]

Much has been written about this rise and fall. Less attention has been paid to the sequence's most remarkable feature, which is the very thing that makes it a sequence rather than a chaotic aggregate of groups, parties, interests, and counterinstitutions, each synchronically related to disparate phenomena elsewhere. This is the tenuous commingling of militant organized labor and Black Power.

The enabling conditions for the sequence, in the first instance, include black labor's simultaneous entry into, and marginalization within, the core of the industrial sector. On the one hand, "the black revolution of the 1960s had finally arrived at one of the most vulnerable links of the American economic system—the point of mass production, the assembly line."[16] On the other, the force of this arrival had been blunted by the traditional unions, whose

---

14   Georgakas and Surkin, *Detroit*, 119.

15   Narrative is assembled from Georgakas and Surkin, *Detroit*; Joshua Bloom and Waldo E. Martin, *Black Against Empire: The History and Politics of the Black Panther Party*, Berkeley: University of California Press, 2013; and A. Muhammad Ahmad, "The League of Revolutionary Black Workers: A Historical Study," historyisaweapon.com.

16   Georgakas and Surkin, *Detroit*, 20.

seniority system effectively gave "legal force to the white male monopoly of the better jobs," in the words of an anonymous author, who continues,

> In this wasteland of labor's twisted hopes, where else could redemption come than from among those whose interests were at every turn sacrificed so that another, more favored group could make its peace with the masters? Where else, indeed, but from among the black workers at the automobile manufacturing infernos of the city of Detroit?[17]

All of this goes toward contextualizing what we might call the "militant black strike." It is a version of the wildcat strike assayed beyond the white-centered traditional unions. It takes its authority in no small part from the urban conflagrations of riot in Detroit and elsewhere—from struggles, that is, not based in shared labor conditions, but rather in a distance from the labor market, in the confrontational struggle for social reproduction outside the sphere of production.

In a similar vein, the riot draws lessons from the tradition of the strike. Writing in the spring of 1967, Black Panther theorist Huey P. Newton is skeptical about the riot:

> We are still in the elementary stage of throwing rocks, sticks, empty wine bottles and beer cans at racist cops who lie in wait for a chance to murder unarmed black people ... We can no longer afford the dubious luxury of the terrible casualties wantonly inflicted upon us by the cops during these rebellions.[18]

---

17 Anonymous worker writing in the *Inner City Voice*, October 1970, cited in Georgakas and Surkin, *Detroit*, 37.

18 Huey P. Newton, *The Huey P. Newton Reader*, eds. David Hilliard and Donald Weise, New York: Seven Stories Press, 2011, 136.

He is no proponent of labor struggles, however. His question is how to pass *through* the riot to more effective combat, and toward this he calls for the "Vanguard Party"—that is to say, toward kinds of order and discipline inherited from the organizing of proletarian labor and agricultural peasantry. It is characteristic of the period that both riot and strike, seeking to overleap their own limits, proceed alongside each other. Each seems to require the other to appear as revolutionary.

This concurrence cannot be recognized as such by official observers. The *Kerner Report*, using the rubric of "disorders," offers this description of the Great Rebellion: "A spirit of carefree nihilism was taking hold. To riot and destroy appeared more and more to become ends in themselves. Late Sunday afternoon it appeared to one observer that the young people were 'dancing amidst the flames.'"[19]

This cannot but harmonize with the "infernos" of labor described above. Everything is burning. Alongside the large-scale increase in black labor, black unemployment after World War II hovers between 150 and 400 percent higher than white, and significantly above nonwhite Hispanic as well.[20] Detroit's overall population peaks in 1950 and begins a fairly steep decline; the city ceases to grow economically around 1960, even as the demographic shift continues.[21] The racial burden of deindustrialization is further freighted by the "last hired, first fired" union policies which reverse the second Great Migration in an

19   Otto Kerner et al., *National Advisory Commission*, 4.
20   Joe T. Darden, Richard C. Hill, and June M. Thomas, *Detroit: Race and Uneven Development*, Philadelphia: Temple University Press, 1990, 107.
21   Campbell Gibson and Kay Jung, "Table 23. Michigan—Race and Hispanic Origin for Selected Large Cities and Other Places: Earliest Census to 1990," PDF, United States Census Bureau, February 2005, census.gov.

ongoing Great Exclusion. Thus we see two trends: a still-dominant manufacturing economy internalizing black labor, but beginning its decline and unable to absorb in full the demographic influx. This implies an increase in both employed and surplus black populations, subject to differential dispossessions. But these tendencies are moving in opposite directions. In the period 1965–1973 the trend lines cross like wires sparking and Detroit sees *the intensification of conditions for both riot and strike,* centered within the black community. This is the situation as the sixties accelerate, and the basis for the political sequence that unfolds, even if it cannot endure.

By 1970, the sequence's opening has already begun to close:

> [The League] believed that the Oakland-based Black Panther Party was moving in the wrong direction by concentrating on organizing lumpen elements of the Black community. The League did not believe that a successful movement could be based upon the lumpen, as they lack a potential source of power. The League believed that Black workers were the most promising base for a successful Black movement because of the potential power derived from ability to disrupt industrial production.[22]

The ideological debate about the proper revolutionary subject (to which we will return), with its seeming regional differences, rests on the fates of the subjects themselves. Already in 1963, Boggs had diagnosed the production of nonproduction and surplus population, and the extent to which it was bound to unmake labor organization. His remarks mark the distance from 1919, when the African

---

22   James A. Geschwender, "The League of Revolutionary Black Workers," *The Journal of Ethnic Studies*, 2: 3, Fall 1974, 9.

Blood Brotherhood (the earliest league of black communists in the U.S.) could include as part of its basic program a demand for "Industrial Development."[23] He writes,

> Automation replaces men. This of course is nothing new. What *is* new is that now, unlike most earlier periods, the displaced men have nowhere to go. The farmers displaced by mechanization of the farms in the 20s could go to the cities and man the assembly line ... in the United States, with automation coming in when industry has already reached the point that it can supply consumer demand, the question of what to do with the surplus people who are the expendables of automation becomes more and more critical every day.[24]

The editors of the special issue are at pains to disagree, insisting that "as productive labor becomes ever more fruitful and less needed," capital will develop other sectors, create "directly and indirectly, other areas of employment —in salesmanship, entertainment, speculation (legal and illegal), personal service, and so on. Some of the jobs thus provided also succumb to automation, but the process of proliferation is not halted."[25] This will have some truth to it; those sectors by and large do see periods of growth as deindustrialization progresses. Not enough, however, to generate the taut labor markets that strikes require—much less to restore capital accumulation at sufficient levels, said labor being largely unproductive in the first place.

Detroit is unique in this period not for the extent to which it is an exception in the historical trajectory of

23   Dawson, *Blacks In and Out*, 50.
24   Boggs, *Boggs Reader*, 102.
25   Leo Huberman and Paul Sweezy, "Editor's Forward," history isaweapon.com.

conditions for riot and strike, but in the way that it is a laboratorial clarification of a dynamic proceeding unevenly across the overdeveloped world, a dynamic based in the great transformation of capitalism that will be known as deindustrialization, accompanied by waning accumulation and changes in the global division of labor and of nonlabor. If militant labor organization seems to prevail in Detroit around 1970, it is in the longer run undermined. By 2005, African Americans will make up more than 80 percent of Detroit's population, and at least one quarter of them will be jobless.[26] Boggs's forecast will in the end capture the reality of the situation.

For all that, it is difficult to emphasize adequately the significance of the effort in this period to merge not just different agendas or goals but different political procedures —to harness riot and strike together, not only as tactics but as modalities.

Riot as Modality

What might it mean, having worked to rearticulate the riot's significance as a form of collective action, to now suggest it is a political modality? For example, what might it mean to suggest that the Panthers are on the side of riot, even if Huey Newton had little faith in such activities? This ambiguity permeates the pages of *The Black Panther* newspaper. A month after the murder of Martin Luther King, Jr. (and the separate police killing of Panther Lil' Bobby Hutton)

---

26 Joe T. Darden and Richard W. Thomas, *Detroit: Race Riots, Racial Conflicts, and Efforts to Bridge the Racial Divide*, East Lansing: Michigan State University Press, 2013, unpaginated, Table 15. Note that all the unemployment data in this chapter is based on the Bureau of Labor Statistics' U3 category, which does not include the underemployed, discouraged from seeking work, incarcerated, and so on. Detroit's full U6 figure in 2005 is probably closer to 45 percent.

and the immediate cascade of riots, Eldridge Cleaver titles his "Dig This" column "Credo for Rioters and Looters" and offers an enthusiastically apocalyptic narrative; the facing page features a large drawing by Matilaba in which two cops arrest or possibly lynch a black youth while three militants with berets, jackets, and rifles ready themselves around a corner. Bold lettering across the illustration's top says "NO MORE RIOTS"; along the side, "TWO'S AND THREE'S."[27]

A first step might be to remark that riot already has a basis in alternative kinds of social cooperation. Robin D. G. Kelley remarks about the Watts uprising of 1965 that "the rebellion grew not from chaos but from a mobilized community" that had hosted a wide array of groups, clubs, more and less formal organizations; as noted above, the same was true in Detroit (and surely elsewhere). In Watts the riots signaled a shift in which "the earlier civil rights orientation gave way to a political culture of Black Power and cultural alternatives to middle-class assimilation." The riots were continuous with a larger political development. So in one case, "soon after the rebellion, radicalized street gangs formed the Sons of Watts and later joined the Black Panther Party."[28]

This continuity between Black Power and riot rests below the surface of policies and plans. They share a circumstance and a purpose: "The riot that's goin' on is a party for self-defense," in the words of Fred Moten, himself a theorist of blackness as surplus.[29] The sense of linkage is perhaps clearer if we return to the baseline formulation

---

27 *The Black Panther*, 2: 2, May 4, 1968: 4–5.

28 Robin D. G. Kelley, "Watts: Remember What They Built, not What They Burned," *Los Angeles Times*, August 11, 2015, latimes.com.

29 Fred Moten, "Necessity, Immensity, and Crisis (Many Edges/ Seeing Things)," *Floor*, 2011. floorjournal.

of riots and strikes as circulation and production struggles respectively. That is what the data of this chapter have been narrating: the initial and veiled decline in U.S. and global production, the germinal shift of bodies and capital into the world of circulation. The political sequence narrates it no less clearly; the status of the riot/strike dynamic in this period serves as a clear window into the period's political economy. Indeed, riot and strike have their full social power because they bear—along with the desires of their participants, their immiserations and negations—the logic of these larger categories. One might say that riot and strike are collective personifications of circulation and production at the limit.

Thus the central passage of the Gwendolyn Brooks poem "Riot," wherein John Cabot of the Brahmin name and luxurious appurtenances, "all whitebluerose below his golden hair," faces his end:

> Because the Negroes were coming down the street.
>
> Because the Poor were sweaty and unpretty
> (not like Two Dainty Negroes in Winnetka)
> and they were coming toward him in rough ranks.
> In seas. In windsweep. They were black and loud.
> And not detainable. And not discreet.[30]

The poem follows the Chicago riots of 1968. There is no labor, only blackness; it is Boggs's future, not his editors'. There is John Cabot's conspicuous consumption, and the unmanageable motion of "the Negroes" through urban passageways. Market and thoroughfare. One could scarcely ask for a better figure of bodies moved into circulation, of circulation as such. The deferred rhyme carries

---

30 Gwendolyn Brooks, *Riot*, Detroit: Broadside Press, 1969, 9.

it, *coming down the street not detainable and not discreet.*
Neither are they discrete. At once ordered and not, "rough
ranks," they become ambient blackness, blackness filling
and overfilling the space of social existence. Cabot prays
that "the blackness" not touch him, but "on It drove /and
breathed on him: and touched him."

It is difficult to discern whether this series of transfers
exists at the level of Cabot's consciousness or of the poem's.
Both, in the end. Cabot is not in fact mistaken about his
fate. Negroes are blackness is riot. At least in 1968. Insofar
as riot is a category recognized by state, law, and market,
blacks coming down the street will always be a riot, or
the moment before, or the moment after. Both socially and
economically, blackness here is surplus—to the state, the
law, the market. It promises always to exceed order, regulation. The riot is an instance of black life in its exclusions
and at the same time in its character as surplus, cordoned
into the noisy sphere of circulation, forced there to defend
itself against the social and bodily death on offer. A surplus
rebellion.

It is no wonder that it provides the basis then for an
imaginary of struggle. This vision circulates in the period's
fiction, which featured "a remarkable proliferation of
novels by African-American authors projecting the possibility of large-scale, catastrophic race war from the mid-1960s
to the early 1970s."[31] This speculative leap might usefully
clarify Newton's position. He is skeptical of the riot's limits,
but for reasons quite contrary to the reasons of those who
insist on the course of labor organization. Newton, no less
than Boggs in his analysis, recognizes that the terrain of
contest marked out by riot is inevitable—that riot is not an

---

31 Julie A. Fiorelli, "Imagination Run Riot: Apocalyptic Race-
War Novels of the Late 1960s," *Mediations*, 28: 1, Fall 2014, 127.

errancy from some true path but exists on the course along which struggle will unfold. It cannot be refused. The riot can do only one thing, and that is expand.

To say that one is lodged within a world in which riot is the form of collective action through which struggle must pass—that it is an *instance* of a full and complex social collectivity—is to encounter riot as social modality. When the material substrate of daily life is the pooling of populations in circulation, in informal economies—a collective population rendered surplus and forced to confront the problem of reproduction in the marketplace rather than in the formal wage—in this situation, any gathering on the corner, in the street, in the square can be understood as a riot. Unlike the strike, it is hard to tell when and where the riot starts and ends. This is part of what allows the riot to function both as a particular event and as a kind of holographic miniature of an entire situation, a world-picture.

If this account seems to aerosolize the riot, this is in keeping with the circumstance *riot prime* confronts. The preindustrial riot finds the market immediately before it, a concrete phenomenon; it finds the economy itself. At the same time it does not find the police, the armed state, except in the most attenuated forms. These technologies of control remain incomplete and at a distance in 1740. Contrarily, the postindustrial riot finds only a sampling of commodities in the local shops. Looting seizes upon this as it must: the truth of the old riot, the setting of prices at zero. As Tom Hayden recognized in the first extended treatment of the 1967 Newark rebellion:

> The riot was more effective against gouging merchants than organized protest had ever been. The year before a survey was started to check on merchants who weighted their

scales. The survey collapsed because of disinterest: people needed power, not proof.[32]

It remains a core activity, clearly continuous with the interventions of the eighteenth century. Nonetheless, the new riot discovers, as it goes to set the price of goods, that the economy as such has receded into planetary logistics and the global division of labor into the ether of finance. The police, however, are to be found on every corner.

The distance between riot and *riot prime,* the two emissaries of circulation struggles, thus seems at first to be the difference between price-setting and not, or between struggle in the market and struggle with the state. These aspects, we have been suggesting, are not so easily separated, either practically or theoretically. In considering the new riot, Georgakas and Surkin conclude that

> The violence of 1967 was significantly different from that of the earlier Detroit explosions. The riots of 1833, 1863, and 1943 had been conflicts between the races. The 1967 Rebellion was a conflict between blacks and state power. In 1943, whites were on the offensive and rode around town in cars looking for easy black targets. In 1967, blacks were on the offensive and their major target was property. In some neighborhoods, Appalachians, students, and other whites took part in the action alongside blacks as their partners. Numerous photos show systematic and integrated looting, which the rebels called "shopping for free."[33]

Janet Abu-Lughod notes that this shift in the object of the riot also describes the rebellions in Harlem and Watts,

---

32 Tom Hayden, *Rebellion in Newark: Official Violence and Ghetto Response,* New York: Random House, 1967, 30.

33 Georgakas and Surkin, *Detroit,* 155.

while insisting that those were "not just about police brutality, however. Both occurred in the context of an economic recession whose effect appeared first in black areas but subsequently spread to the wider U.S. economy," just as in Detroit.[34]

In short, the conceptual distinction between state and economic violence is elusive. Guy Debord, assessing the Watts rebellion, theorizes the double confrontation with state and property and their changing positions. "Society finds in looting its *natural* response to the unnatural and inhuman abundance of commodities," he writes. This has been consistently misunderstood as suggesting that looting is a hyperbolic realization of consumer ideology (a common refrain from liberal commentators), despite what Debord says immediately after: "It [looting] instantly undermines the commodity as such, and it also exposes its ultimate logic: the army, the police and the other specialized forces possessed of the state's monopoly on armed violence."[35] Perhaps this exposure is the purpose of looting, as Bruno Bosteels has argued, should one seek in French theory the discursive import of riot.[36] At the same time, looting is certainly continuous with the practical history of price-setting. Either way, Debord captures something about the overdeveloped world and its apparent abstraction. The police now stand *in the place of* the economy, the violence of the commodity made

---

34 Abu-Lughod, *Race, Space*, 25.

35 Guy Debord, "Le déclin et la chute de l'économie spectaculaire-marchande," *Internationale Situationiste 1958–69: Édition augementée*, Paris: Librarie Arthème Fayard, 2004, 418. Translation my own. This essay was unsigned in the original, but later credited to Guy Debord.

36 Bruno Bosteels, *Marx and Freud in Latin America: Politics, Psychoanalysis, and Religion in Times of Terror*, London: Verso, 2012, 292.

flesh. In the burning world of the last instance they are fungible:

> What is a policeman? He is the commodity's active servant, the man fully subsumed by the commodity, by whose efforts a given product of human labor remains a commodity with the magical property of being paid for, not merely a refrigerator or rifle—something blind, passive, insensate, subject to the first person ready to make use of it. Behind the humiliation of being subject to police, Blacks reject the humiliation of being subject to commodities.[37]

The simplest formula is this. For riot, the economy is near, the state far. For *riot prime*, the economy is far, the state near. Either way it is the marketplace and the street. *Hic Rhodus, hic salta!*

---

37   Debord, "Déclin," 418.

PART 3: RIOT PRIME

CHAPTER 7

The Long Crisis

Riot and crisis arrive together, each the herald of the other. The new era of riot comes into its own not only with the intensification of urban and then suburban rebellions but with the eclipse of worker's movements, the trend lines of riot and strike first crossing and then diverging in time with the peak and decline of the "long twentieth century" of American hegemony. What has crisis to do with riot, beyond this coincidence and some anxiously diaphanous sense of things falling apart?

The deep relation of riot and crisis is the concern of what remains of this book, not least because of our core argument: *crisis signals a shift of capital's center of gravity into circulation, both theoretically and practically, and riot is in the last instance to be understood as a circulation struggle, of which the price-setting struggle and the surplus rebellion are distinct, if related, forms.* In the foregoing chapters this has been hazarded piecemeal and now deserves a systematic unfolding. This is peculiarly necessary, given that crisis most often appears as a punctual event, even as it expresses an underlying and ongoing process in which capital encounters its internal limits and struggles violently in order to overcome them. Crisis is the exclamation point of profound social reorganization. Riots express this changed social organization, address themselves to it, and seek to abolish it and thus themselves.

The Long Downturn, to take up Brenner's language, is similar to previous declines. This book argues nonetheless that the past four decades might be understood somewhat differently as a Long Crisis. The current period is distinguished from similar passages in previous cycles to the extent that recoveries of the sort seen previously remain from our vantage invisible. Historically, capital has resolved its unfolding contradiction by relocating elsewhere, seeking out a circumstance where production has not yet undermined itself and the accumulation process can begin again on a new and expanded basis. This has the effect of restabilizing the capitalist world-system volatilized by secular crisis. It is not at all clear that this has happened, or is in motion, in the years since the global economic downturn of the late sixties and early seventies. Bids on a new hegemony by East Asian economies and the Eurozone have foundered en route; "emerging economies" appear already too advanced in their productivity to drive accumulation on a global scale by internalizing masses of new labor into industry or the larger category of manufacture.[1] Planetary malaise persists, and volatility with it.

This does not mean that relocations and restorations of capital accumulation are impossible. Only at one's peril does one make strong claims about a historical period while still within it. Thus these remarks must be somewhat provisional, an attempt to develop a reasonably unified account of the era. There is, at least, some agreement about where to start.

"What about 1973–4, then?" wondered Fernand Braudel, great historian of the *longue durée*. The year 1973 sees the first in a series of oil shocks, the formal withdrawal of

---

1   See Joshua Clover and Aaron Benanav, "Can Dialectics Break BRICS?" *The South Atlantic Quarterly* 113: 4, Fall 2014, 743–59.

the U.S. from its Southeast Asian adventure, and the final collapse of the Bretton Woods monetary system setting the stage for increasing trade and current account imbalances; concomitant with these is a global downturn of markets. This is a bare beginning of the ledger. "Is this a short term conjunctural crisis, as most economists seem to think? Or have we had the rare and unenviable privilege of seeing with our own eyes the century begin its turn?"[2]

The questions are rhetorical. Braudel is assessing "secular cycles," the longest of economic periods—what Arrighi would clarify as cycles of accumulation led by a state capable of driving material expansion of a world-economy, over which the leading nation achieves hegemony to the extent that its gains are part of systemic profits (and to the extent that it is able to guarantee stability to the interstate system). Both writers reach back to protocapitalist commercial empires for a consideration of four ever-larger and ever-swifter but similarly patterned cycles. For Braudel, one cycle begins as another ends, in the manner of monarchical reigns. In Arrighi's revised account, they overlap, one hegemon riding its twilight phase of financialization downward to darkness on extended credit even as it finances a rising hegemon's acceleration toward industrial takeoff.

Inevitably, "1973" is a metonym for changes too capacious for a single year to contain. Nonetheless, this dating of "the point at which the secular trend begins to go into decline, in other words, the moment of crisis" has become a matter of broad agreement among historians and theorists of the *longue durée*, relatively small differences notwithstanding.[3] We have already encountered the most dramatic fact, from the perspective of accumulation and hegemony:

2 Fernand Braudel, *The Perspective of the World: Civilisation and Capitalism*, vol. 3, Berkeley: University of California Press, 1982, 80.

3 Ibid., 77.

the secular collapse in profitability and growth, led by the decline of U.S. manufacturing, such that the best years of the downturn are worse than the best years of the boom (with only one or two minor exceptions). We might therefore date the cyclical ascent of finance back to this moment, though not because financial has "pushed out" industrial capital—a conceptual model opening onto the catastrophic idea of good and bad capitalism, or healthy and unhealthy capitalism. Capital is a unitary space of flows seeking investment opportunities that will return the average profit rate. When this requirement can no longer be satisfied by a growing industrial sector, profits are stored in safe havens, or reinvested elsewhere in commercial enterprise and/or financial instruments. Financialization is simply the name for this shift in capital flows. When we note the publication of the most celebrated piece of financial engineering, the Black-Scholes option pricing model, or the opening of the first major derivatives market, the Chicago Board Options Exchange, both in 1973, we must be clear that these are not new artillery that allow the forces of finance to batter down the walls of industry. They are consequences of capital's need for room to move beyond the industrial sector.

The Arc of Accumulation

Crisis theory addresses the question of why industrial expansion must end and give way to the speculative longueurs of finance in a great redirection of capital flows punctuated by a massive devaluation of value. Arrighi and Brenner, arguably the two most cogent economic historians of the passage peaking in 1973, provide diverging explications of this particular waning of accumulation, based on their differing senses of what capitalism is; both also diverge in some details from Marx's abstract theory of crisis.

Arrighi's model is undertheorized, in keeping with his more descriptive account of world-economies. He implies a somewhat eclectic causality relying on a largely Smithian theory of crisis premised on market competition that steadily erodes profit margin. Labor struggles (understood in the manner of Karl Polanyi) offer another squeeze on profits, as does the expense of hegemonic duties as global constable. These motivate investment away from the beleaguered state-industrial nexus toward the international financial markets.

Brenner's more systematic theorization rests on a model of overproduction in which unchallenged U.S. industrial capacity after World War II eventually confronts competition from more efficient international producers, notably Germany and Japan. With high levels of investment sunk already in fixed capital, the value of which can only be recouped through further commodity manufacture, U.S. firms are unable to scale back on production and so are locked into fratricidal competition for market share. Firms that should be washed out of a sector in a flood of creative destruction meant to open channels for new growth instead stagger onward, often supported by the state, which requires their wealth and labor management for its stability. This leads to "what was effectively a process of overinvestment leading to overcapacity and overproduction in manufacturing on an international scale," initiating systemic turbulence that has not subsided yet.[4]

Both of these analyses remain at the level of price, the quantitative level that describes the effective manifestation of crisis. For Marx's value analysis, the movements

---

4 Brenner, *Turbulence*, 38.

of profits are surface phenomena corresponding to an underlying shift in the balance of constant to variable capital: means of production to waged labor, or dead to living labor. Despite countervailing forces, this so-called organic composition of capital tends to rise over time as competition compels increasing productivity, iteratively replacing labor with more efficient machines and labor processes (what the twentieth century knew as Fordism and Taylorism respectively).

This increasing domination of dead over living labor is an expression throughout the social whole of the law of value, as increasing productivity decreases the average amount of socially necessary labor time required to produce commodities. The economic consequences proceed unevenly. Initially, increases in productivity generate high profits that draw further investment and more labor into production. These, in combination, produce further expansion. Over time, however, the rise in the ratio of dead to living labor undermines the capacity for value production, living labor in the production process being the sole source of surplus value. The same dynamic that originally drives accumulation—increasing productivity at the nexus of wage and commodity—also undermines it, until manufacturing capacity and labor capacity can no longer be brought together, and instead empty factories and unemployed populations pile up side by side. This expanded process we call the *production of nonproduction*. Crisis and decline come not from extrinsic shocks but from capital's internal limits. We might call this the "arc of accumulation" that charts the contradictions of capital along the axis of historical time. To call it an arc doubtless smooths a jagged ride.[5]

---

5 For one image of the ratcheting movement of accumulation and crisis, see Henryk Grossman, *Law of Accumulation and Breakdown of the Capitalist System*, London: Pluto Press, 1992, 84.

Moreover, the plot does not express some simply quantitative fact about growth rates or the like. The two sides of the arc, although still arrangements of capitalism and expressions of the value dynamic, are qualitatively different in their social organization in a dialectic of continuity and rupture.

In the long twentieth century, the arc of accumulation has seen first the "unprecedented transfer of population from agriculture to industry," and then, in a great reversal, deindustrialization moving population out of industry and out of the production process more generally into either service work or under- and unemployment.[6] These are social reorganizations on a global scale.

Despite their differing analyses of causation both Brenner and Arrighi succeed in excavating the strong relation between the *logical* account of self-undermining accumulation and the *historical* account of capitalist cycles, particularly of the current cycle on which they focus. That is, for all its metaphysical subtleties, the debate regarding the so-called Law of the Tendency of the Rate of Profit to Fall has a sufficient correspondence to the rises and falls that Arrighi has brought forth so comprehensively. Arrighi's account begins with Marx's formula for expanded reproduction of capital, MCM´ (money-capital-money´): money's compulsory itinerary from the perspective of the capitalist, passing into commodity production if and only if the resulting commodities can be sold at a higher price— for the capitalist remains a capitalist only if this can be arranged. Arrighi's novelty is then to displace this logical process onto the empirical history of his "long centuries."

6 Aaron Benanav and John Clegg, "Misery and Debt: On the Logic and History of Surplus Populations and Surplus Capital," *Contemporary Marxist Theory*, eds. Andrew Pendakis et al., New York: Bloomsbury, 2014, 585.

He identifies "the alternation of epochs of material expansion (MC phases of capital accumulation) with phases of financial rebirth and expansion (CM′ phases)." He narrates this phase shift via his temporal opposition of MC and CM′ periods:

> In phases of material expansion money capital "sets in motion" an increasing mass of commodities (including commoditized labor-power and gifts of nature); and in phases of financial expansion an increasing mass of money capital "sets itself free" from its commodity form, and accumulation proceeds through financial deals (as in Marx's abridged formula MM′). Together, the two epochs or phases constitute a full systemic cycle of accumulation (MCM′).[7]

In the age of modern capitalism, this phase of material expansion is cognate with industrial growth. In such a phase, the main action is the purchase of labor power and of means of production toward the making of commodities— that is to say, valorization within the production process. In the period of financial expansion, the main action is the sale of these commodities toward realization of the value they bear—that is, capital recenters on the marketplace, on exchange and consumption. This is the sense of an era of circulation from the perspective of capital: as production's capacity for generating high profits declines, capital shifts its investments toward realization in the immediate present of both extant value, and of value allegedly waiting to be generated in the future.

This might be formulated differently. Crisis bursts forth at the moment that profit and expectation of profit cease flowing from manufacturing. In that moment, creditors seek

---

7 Arrighi, *Long Twentieth Century*, 87.

to collect on their debts before the debtors become destitute; debtor firms are in turn compelled to cease reinvesting in production while frantically hawking their wares in the marketplace to meet their obligations. Or we might narrate matters as previously mentioned: the money available for reinvestment ceases moving when manufacturing profits fall below a certain threshold, and increasingly comes to rest in banks, marking time while awaiting sufficiently tempting investment opportunities. This moment of immobility is the moment of crisis; when capital begins to move again, it seeks out both commerce and claims on future value, what Marx calls fictitious capital. A suggestive example from the present era is the extent to which surviving U.S. automakers increasingly derive profits not from production but from financing consumer purchases through in-house credit arms. Again we see that financial expansion is industrial contraction viewed from a different position. And again we have narrated in different terms the same shift from valorization to realization, production to circulation.

Modern capitalism has seen two arcs, British and U.S.-centered, the latter rising as the former declines. Each has its own particularities. They can at the same time be synthesized into one longer arc. From the first takeoff until the recent decline there has always been an engine of global accumulation churning away. From roughly 1830 to 1973 there was a core of productive capital in the west with its ratcheting systemic expansion. It is according to this that we earlier called the period from the eighteenth century to the present a metacycle, a great arc of accumulation in the capitalist world-system following the course of *circulation-production-circulation prime*.

The period of *circulation prime*, the social reorganization of Long Crisis, conditions the decline of the strike and the new era of riots in two distinct if inevitably related ways: the spatialization of the economy, and the recomposition of the capital/class relation. Let us take them one at a time, before reuniting them at the end.

The Spatialization of Struggle

Riots are originally struggles over the price of goods, that is, struggles over reproduction outside the wage but still suspended in the market. They are "struggles to control space" and passage through it; there is a slant rhyme between the paradigmatic export riot at King's Lynn in 1347 and the massive blockade at the Port of Oakland in 2011.[8] The control over space takes many forms, often involving efforts to drive police from the commercial districts they defend. Riots are obsessed with buildings, with plazas and passages, with massing in the square and the streets. Hobsbawm devotes a chapter of his book *Revolutionaries* to urbanism's role in insurrection. There is something architectural about a riot, which is to say spatial. The barricade, that great instrument of riot, finds its origins in the chaining off of neighborhoods against incursion; the rise of the barricade is nothing but the rise of the first era of riot, receding after the Spring of Nations in 1848.[9] The new wide boulevards of the nineteenth century are, in telling after telling, designed to bring an end to barricade and riot both; industrial growth will in the end do a better job of it.

The practical spatiality of riot corresponds to a theoretical distinction. The abstract logic of production is temporal, the abstract logic of circulation spatial. Production is organized by value, by the valorization of commodities, and this

---

8 Abu-Lughod, *Race, Space,* 41.

9 Mark Traugott, *The Insurgent Barricade*, Berkeley: University of California Press, 2010, 81–82.

value is regulated by the socially necessary labor time. It is through this time that both sides reproduce themselves. In production, both capital and its antagonists struggle over this time—its duration, its price. The strike is a temporal struggle.

Once the temporal value of living labor comes to rest in the commodity, it becomes objectified, spatialized. Circulation is organized by price, by the realization of surplus value as profit when commodities exchange places. This is a conceptually thorny formulation, as is apparent from Marx's exposition:

> Money is now *objectified* labor, whether it possesses the form of money or of a particular commodity. No objective mode of being of labor is opposed to capital, but all of them appear as possible modes of existence for it, which it can assume through a simple change in form, going from the money form over into the commodity form. The only antithesis to *objectified* labor is *unobjectified* labor; in antithesis to *objectivized* labor, subjectified labor. Or that labor that is present in time, living, in antithesis to labor past in time, but existing in space. As labor that is present in time, unobjectified (and thus also not yet objectified), this can only be present as *capacity*, possibility, ability, as *labor-capacity* of the living subject.[10]

In thinking through the logical relationship of labor and commodities, Marx arrives at the antithesis of unobjectified and objectified labor. On the one side, labor power

---

10   Karl Marx, "Fragment des Urtexts von 'Zur Kritik der politischen Ökonomie,'" *Grundrisse der Kritik der Politischen Ökonomie*, Berlin: Dietz Verlag, 1858/1953, 942 (emphasis in original). Cited in Jacques Camatte, *Capital and Community: The Results of the Immediate Process of Production and the Economic Work of Marx*, trans. David Brown, London: Unpopular Books, 1988, 20.

which has not yet been transferred to a commodity in the production process; on the other, the value objectified in commodities that now enter into the space of circulation, themselves spatial objects. The rise in the ratio of constant to variable capital, dead to living labor, is the process of spatialization itself, and thus the transformation of temporal to spatial struggles.

This distinction exists at the practical level as well, regarding circulation in the concrete sense: transport, communications, finance. Marx famously speaks of "the annihilation of space by time." This has often been understood as asserting the growing irrelevance of spatial relations to capital. The opposite is the case. Marx argues that space presents itself as the fundamental problem for exchange, and the more capital rests on exchange, the more space poses problems to be overcome:

> Capital by its nature drives beyond every spatial barrier. Thus the creation of the physical conditions of exchange— of the means of communication and transport—the annihilation of space by time—becomes an extraordinary necessity for it. Only insofar as the direct product can be realized in distant markets in mass quantities in proportion to reductions in the transport costs, and only insofar as at the same time the means of communication and transport themselves can yield spheres of realization for labor, driven by capital; only insofar as commercial traffic takes place in massive volume—in which more than necessary labor is replaced—only to that extent is the production of cheap means of communication and transport a condition for production based on capital, and promoted by it for that reason.[11]

---

11   Marx, *Grundrisse*, 524–5 (emphasis in original).

Readers will likely know the often tedious debates about whether this passage suggests that circulation is internalized to production, or whether this is only an appearance and the works and wares of circulation are, as Marx continues, "a *condition* for the production process"—a quite different claim.[12] For our purposes, the significance is the same. This is particularly the case as we are not claiming that struggles in circulation have privileged relation to value production. In the shift that follows crisis, capital, unable to generate adequate surplus value or growth through conventional manufacturing production, is compelled into the space of circulation to compete for profits there, by decreasing its costs and increasing turnover time for an ever greater volume of commodities. Struggles in this space are thus central to each given capital's ongoing existence. There is scant intimation that this generates accumulation in the manner of industrial production.

And yet this is the unmistakable fate of capital post-1973, rendering "our present as fundamentally a *time* of *logistics space.*"[13] This systemic reorganization, Jasper Bernes notes, "indexes the subordination of production to the conditions of circulation, the becoming-hegemonic of those aspects of the production process that involve circulation." There will be implications in this development for contemporary struggles. "Logistics is capital's art of war, a series of techniques for intercapitalist and interstate competition."[14] It will require a counterart that adapts itself to this transformed terrain but one that also recognizes

12   Ibid., 525 (emphasis in original).

13   Deborah Cowen, *The Deadly Life of Logistics: Mapping Violence in Global Trade*, Minneapolis: University of Minnesota Press, 2014, 5 (emphases in original).

14   Jasper Bernes, "Logistics, Counterlogistics and the Communist Prospect," *Endnotes* 3, 2013, 185.

logistics space as peculiarly structured by capital's needs, the sort of machinery that the proletariat may not simply lay hold of and wield for its own purposes.

The massive finance-fueled build-out of global shipping and containerization, arguably the single most foundational project for capital in the era, signals the sea change. It is presaged by the regularization of intermodal shipping containers (having been perfected to address logistical problems of the Vietnam War) via a series of agreements from 1968 to 1970 and deregulation of transport in the following decade.[15] The Center for Transportation & Logistics is established at the Massachusetts Institute of Technology in 1973: "a world leader in supply chain management education and research."[16] Just-In-Time manufacturing, which becomes generalized in the seventies, is the methodological aspect of the same change. Developed in the Japanese auto industry, it is the other of the U.S. auto industry's Fordist paradigm, discovering efficiencies less in the organization of production than in circulation, inventory, exchange: an interlocking set of practices the core of which constitutes a kind of supply-chain Taylorism.

The correspondence of these developments with industrial crisis verges on absolute. Expressions of this interlocking motion are numerous. In April 1973, Federal Express delivers its first package; forty years into the Long Crisis, FedEx will have the fourth-largest fleet and be by freight the largest airline in the world.[17]

---

15 Marc Levinson, *The Box: How the Shipping Container Made the World Smaller and the World Economy Bigger*, Princeton: Princeton University Press, 2006, 147–9.

16 See the MIT Center for Transportation & Logistics MIT website, ctl.mit.edu.

17 See the About FedEx webpage, "Our Story: History and Timeline," about.van.fedex.com; and the IATA Publications and Interactive Tools webpage, http://web.archive.org/web/20120427115854/

The End of the Program

The circulatory shift is an economic restructuring that both drives and rests on a massive social reorganization, a recomposition of capital and class. This transforms the political horizons profoundly, and with them the forms of struggle. The underlying changes have proved opaque to some observers. One, writing in the democratic socialist journal *Jacobin*, discovers in 2015 that "the U.S. economy revolves around the sprawling logistics industry" and can conclude only, "after three decades of gut-wrenching changes to the industrial economy, I believe that socialists can, once again, have an industrial strategy in the United States."[18] Another proffer from the same venue notices the same transformation "particularly in lean production and just-in-time inventories," and recognizes the resulting importance of "focusing on these distribution points" so as to "blockade distribution." The author recommends toward this purpose the organization of "strategically placed groups of workers."

These instances correctly recognize the vast transfer of labor from industrial production into the space of circulation, distribution, exchange. However, the significance of this as an aspect of a thoroughgoing social restructuring is neglected. One could forgive a reader for being perplexed as to why the hollowing out of the industrial sector, the historical basis for socialist organizing, would call for "an industrial strategy" once again. One might in turn ask why "blockading distribution," precisely the tactic of nonworkers both logically and historically, demands "groups of workers." From this perspective, no matter the problem,

---

http://www.iata.org/ps/publications/pages/wats-freight-km.aspx.

18   Joe Allen, "Studying Logistics," *Jacobin*, February 12, 2015, jacobinmag.com.

the solution is always the same: industrial labor organization. It is always the time of strike.

One might argue that circulation workers are somehow more difficult to organize, that something peculiar to the new workplace excludes the possibility. There are reasons to believe such a thing. In addition to disaggregation and deskilling as barriers to organization, the traditional downing of tools presupposes a sense of moral possession by the workers of their equipment, a remnant of artisanal and craft cultures that provides a legitimating function alien to the realm of circulation. That said, there is no argument here against such organizing. The 1997 UPS strike shows such things are possible. It is inevitable that a growing percentage of the vanishingly few strikes will be in circulation, and that labor actions will shift toward circulation struggles, as a practical matter. Consider the illustrative tactical shift on the part of French trade unions, for example when French oil refineries and petroleum depots were blockaded for two weeks in 2010.[19] More broadly, normative arguments about what people who struggle *should* do miss the most basic truth. People will struggle where they are.

Our argument is that people are somewhere else. And further that the explosion of such workplaces is symptomatic of a larger restructuring which augurs poorly for the potential of such organizing. Labor in the overdeveloped world has not simply shifted its center of gravity in some neutral sense. Its relation to accumulation is profoundly changed, and against this change a demand for unchanged forms of action seems at best a failure of understanding. A class politics of even the most recondite or reductionist variety is now compelled to refigure itself according to

19 For a comprehensive study of this phenomenon in relation to riots, see Blaumachen, "The Transitional Phase of the Crisis: The Era of Riots," blaumachen.gr.

these great political-economic transformations or consign itself to the endless role-playing of a backdated romance to which the perfume of 1917 always clings.

Jacobin editor Bhaskar Sunkara summarizes these ritualistic politics. He recognizes that it "might be helpful to consider the ways in which the current situation resembles a *return* to pre-Fordism"; given the resemblance, the politics on offer then must surely still obtain, and "sometimes new crises have to be confronted with old vocabulary."[20] But which old vocabulary is that, and why would it demand the same set of strategies these thinkers have been propounding for more than a century without variation? We might note here a simple error in grasping the character of the arc of accumulation. It supposes that a point on the descent would be historically identical to a point on the ascent simply because they were at the same height (of profit or unemployment rate, etc.). This misprision does not take into account the vector: the difference between rise and fall, between tightening and slackening labor markets, between the capacity for dynamism and expansion and the course of stagnation and contraction. The conditions that historically enable the socialist vocabulary—real accumulation, a taut labor market, the possibility of gaining power by appropriating a share of that accumulation, an expanding industrial proletariat—no longer obtain. The progressive gains that might empower and embolden the mass party depending on labor organizing are no longer within reach as they were during economic growth, expansion, and boom. This is part of a broader shift: "The year 1978," as a business historian succinctly noted, was "Waterloo for unions, regulators, Keynesian tax reformers."[21]

---

20 Bhaskar Sunkara, "Precarious Thought," *Jacobin*, January 13, 2012, jacobinmag.com.

21 Jefferson Cowie, *Stayin' Alive: The 1970s and the Last Days of*

Perhaps we might concede that Sunkara is half right. It is inevitably the case that we will understand new moments first through old vocabularies. But we are farther along the arc than he can suppose, and so might need to reach back for a rather older lexicon and make it new. It is earlier than we think. Which is to say, it is a good deal later.

The waning of the labor movement in the west needs little narration here. Counternarratives, particularly those that suggest the decline results from ideological combat, failures of will, or strategic errors, have by now been subjected to what Marx called the practical criticism of the real. The basic data are well known. Arguably the clearest is the collapse toward zero of strikes involving more than 1,000 workers beginning in the late seventies. For those skeptical of that measure (which correlates poorly with unionization), the situation might be rendered thus: in the United States after 1981, only three years exceed 10 million cumulative days idle from strike actions, with several years below 1 million. From 1947 to 1981, the figure exceeds 10 million every single year, averaging more than twice that.[22]

We might find a decisive moment by returning once more to Detroit and to 1973, where "for the first time in the history of the UAW, the union mobilized to keep a plant open."[23] This will swiftly become the paradigm for labor organizing, wanted or not. With the hollowing-out of the

---

the Working Class, New York: New Press, 2010, 292. The cited source is Kim McQuaid, *Uneasy Partners: Big Business in American Politics, 1945–1990*, Baltimore: Johns Hopkins University Press, 1994, 156.

22   See the Bureau of Labor Statistics' online database, "Economic News Release: Table 1. Work stoppages involving 1,000 or more workers, 1947–2014" (version updated February 11, 2015), bls.gov.

23   Bill Bonds, WXYZ-TV News, speaking of events at the Mack stamping plant, August 16, 1973. Cited in Georgakas and Sunkin, *Detroit*, 189.

industrial sector and the loss of profitability, the main threat for both capital and labor is that a given firm will cease to exist. And, at a larger scale, that capital's own capacity for self-reproduction will collapse. From that point on, struggles against capital can only be *against* capital's existence, rather than *for* the empowering of labor. Capital and labor find themselves now in collaboration to preserve capital's self-reproduction, to preserve the labor relation along with the firm's viability. This provides near-absolute limits for bargaining.

We might call it "the affirmation trap," in which labor is locked into the position of affirming its own exploitation under the guise of survival. It is a version of what Lauren Berlant calls "cruel optimism." Optimism is cruel in an ever more common situation:

> The object/scene that ignites a sense of possibility actually makes it impossible to attain the expansive transformation for which a person or a people risks striving; and, doubly, it is cruel insofar as the very pleasures of being inside a relation have become sustaining regardless of the content of the relation.[24]

Surely this describes with exactitude not just any relation, but the exigencies of the labor relation in the Long Crisis. The affirmation trap is cruel optimism at its most obdurate stratum, existing independently of libidinal attachments, its compulsions involving no misrecognition. The sustaining pleasures are food and shelter.

Caught in the affirmation trap, labor ceases to be the antithesis of capital. This might be seen as the ironic endgame of the very affirmation that defines the socialist

---

24 Lauren Berlant, *Cruel Optimism* Durham: Duke University Press, 2011, 2.

horizon of struggle, in which "revolution is thus the affirmation of the proletariat, whether as a dictatorship of the proletariat, workers' councils, the liberation of work, a period of transition, the withering of the state, generalized self-management, or a 'society of associated producers.'"[25]

These are the terms in which the group Théorie Communiste defines "programmatism," the central model of class-based revolutionary struggle in the twentieth century. Moishe Postone identifies programmatism (he does not use the term) with "traditional Marxism" that, he argues, misrecognizes the basis of capitalism as ownership of the means of production, while treating productive labor as "the transhistorical source of wealth and the basis of social constitution." Seizure of the means of production therefore preserves the capitalist *form of wealth* while redistributing it socially, and so "traditional Marxism replaces Marx's critique of the mode of production and distribution with a critique of the mode of distribution alone."[26] Thus the distinction used here between socialism and communism: the former indicating this distributionist model, the latter indicating the abolition of the economy and the end of the indexical relation between one's labor and any relation or access to social wealth.

This "traditional Marxism" must be taken historically. The socialist horizon of programmatism should not be understood as an analytical or moral failing, nor as a kind of stopping short; there would be a passage from socialism to communism (or from a lower to higher phase of communism, as Marx has it in *Critique of the Gotha Program*). Rather, it accurately refracts the real conditions of the

---

25 Théorie Communiste, "Much Ado About Nothing," *Endnotes* 1, 2008, 155.

26 Moishe Postone, *Time, Labor, and Social Domination*, Cambridge: Cambridge University Press, 1993, 69 (emphasis in original).

world in which it arises. It is a struggle against capital "seen from the point of view of the worker, i.e., from the point of view of the cycle of productive capitalism," in the words of Gilles Dauvé.[27] That is to say, it arises with the rising power of industrial labor, which is why workers in this sector are able to stand as the revolutionary class fraction. Their growth is capital's expansion. This does not, however, imply an immutable standpoint or form of struggle: "the centrality of proletarian labor to Marx's analysis of capitalism should not be taken as an affirmative evaluation on his part of its ontological primacy to social life, or as part of an argument that workers are the most oppressed group in society."[28]

It is from the far side of accumulation's rainbow that programmatism's historical limits become evident. When the class fraction that centered the program era no longer exerts a peculiar power over capital, such a course of struggle is foreclosed. This outcome is not the consequence of political wiles, of some nefarious policy deployment under the heading of "neoliberalism." It is capital's own self-transformation from the perspective of labor—labor forced now to affirm capital in the same gesture through which it affirms its own being. It is precisely this struggle for self-preservation, what Théorie Communiste calls "class belonging as an external constraint," which is the limit for labor struggles as revolutionary engine.[29] Wage demands, once imagined to offer advantage or even leverage toward

---

27   Gilles Dauvé, *Ni Parlement ni syndicats: les Conseils ouvriers*, Paris: Editions Les Nuits rouges, 2008, 6.

28   Postone, *Social Domination*, 356 n.120.

29   Théorie Communiste, "Communization in the Present Tense," *Communization and Its Discontents: Contestation, Critique, and Contemporary Struggles,* ed. Benjamin Noys, Wivenhoe: Minor Compositions, 2011, 53.

the abolition of class, must now be fitted to the needs of capital's self-reproduction as that self-reproduction enters into crisis. In its twilit lassitude, the working class is reduced to reproducing little beyond the conditions of its own immiseration. The wage struggle retains its legitimacy as a claim on survival—*wage, wage against the dying of the light*—but at the same time legitimates capital. It has no beyond.

Overdetermination

The riot seeks to preserve nothing, to affirm nothing but for perhaps a shared antagonist, a shared misery, a shared negation. It lacks a program. Under the heading "This was not a movement," one commentator on the 2011 London riots writes,

> In the August unrest, nothing in the situation of its protagonists was worth defending: neighborhood, residency, community, ethnicity and race, were all revealed as aspects of capital's reproduction, which produces these proletarians as actual paupers ... The language of the riots was not the positive language of the "movement," social change, demands or politics, but the negative language of vandalism. What happened was a lot of destruction, nothing was built, no plans, no strategies.[30]

This is for many observers riot's most unsettling characteristic. In the face of this, the demand for a program, the demand for demands, is itself a familiar demand, the death rattle of prescriptive politics. It will not be met. But this

---

30 Rocamadur/Blaumachen, "The Feral Underclass Hits the Streets: On the English Riots and Other Ordeals," *SIC*, no. 2, January 2014, 113–4.

is not to say riot lacks determinations. In fact, the riot is astonishingly overdetermined by the array of historical transformations that make the particular genre of antagonism we call circulation struggles inevitable.

A summary will be useful. The social surplus accompanying accumulation has dwindled, and with it the capacity of capital and state to meet demands for both direct and social wages, occasional exceptions notwithstanding. The wage demand is foreclosed as anything but a rearguard action inseparable from the affirmation of capital's being. Capital has shifted its hopes for profit into the space of circulation, and thus shifted its vulnerability there. Labor has shifted into circulation with it. So has nonlabor: the under- and unemployed, those left to informal economies, those left to molder. This deindustrialization has been dramatically racialized.

The death of the wage demand spells the fading of production struggles unified by the participants' shared role as wage labor. At the same time, the circulation struggle has no logical requirement that its participants be workers. If labor has the immediate access and legitimacy to interrupt production in the factory, anyone can liberate a marketplace, close a road, close a port. As in the eighteenth century, rioters may be workers, but they do not appear *as* workers; participants are not unified by their possession of jobs but by their more general dispossession. Into the space of the market they go, struggling for reproduction beyond the wage. This is the definition we offered in the introduction, come round again.

Perhaps, then, "overdetermination" gets it wrong. A new situation for social contest has been generated. A new arrangement of population through the same motion generates circulation workers and nonworkers, who happen to share a relation to that situation of contest. This shift in forms of collective action is one of dialectical deftness. But the dialectic needs the proletariat, and have we not just declared the working class dead?

CHAPTER 8

Surplus Rebellions

There is much conjecture, some of it government-funded, on how riots spread.[1] This is true in no small part because individual instances are subject to real contingencies and local determinations; mechanistic explanations generate their own exceptions as swiftly as they do confirmations. The most common language is that of contagion, the vectors being individual agents or mass media. In 1793, William Godwin wrote,

> The conviviality of feast may lead to the depredation of riot. The sympathy of opinion catches from man to man, especially in numerous meetings, and among persons whose passions have not been used to the curb of judgment ... There is nothing more barbarous, bloodthirsty and unfeeling than the triumph of a mob.[2]

Two centuries later, the authors of *The Coming Insurrection* propose that "revolutionary movements do not spread by contamination but by resonance."[3]

---

1 For example, The U.S. Department of Defense–funded Minerva Institute. See "Program History and Overview," minerva.dtic.mil.

2 William Godwin, *Enquiry Concerning Political Justice and its Influence on Morals and Happiness*, vol. I, London: G.G.J. and J. Robinson, 1793, 208.

3 Invisible Committee, *Coming Insurrection*, 12 (emphasis in original).

Sam Greenlee's 1969 novel *The Spook Who Sat by the Door* contains a vision of the race riot transcending its spatial barriers and becoming a guerilla race-war that threatens the nation-state. "Oakland blew first, then Los Angeles, then, leap-frogging the continent, Harlem and South Philadelphia ... Every city with a ghetto wondered if they might be next. The most powerful nation in history stood on the brink of panic and chaos."[4] Leaps, leaps, leaps. It is a fiction, of course. Moreover, in Greenlee's story the generalization is orchestrated by Pantherine "Freedom Fighters." This is very much an artifact of 1969, of the idea of the vanguardist party still persisting in that moment. But the implicit logic is less metaphorical than contagion, less idealistic than resonance. Above or below the fiction, Greenlee's account accords with the spread of riots in France in 2005, England in 2011, the U.S. in 2014 and 2015. Riot goes looking for surplus populations, and these are its basis for expansion. This is not to deny the agency of rioters, of looters, of people shooting at cops. Nor is it to suggest that such spreading rebellions have no basis in various kinds of conscious and collective vision. It is simply the same movement seen through the other end of the telescope, seen from the perspective of riot itself. From this perspective, one might begin to synthesize the categories of crisis, surplus population, and race that seem enduring aspects of *riot prime* in the west.

All three aspects are comprehended in Ruth Wilson Gimore's compact summary:

> Crisis is not objectively bad or good, rather, it signals systematic change whose outcome is determined through struggle. Struggle, which is a politically neutral word, occurs at all

---

4 Sam Greenlee, *The Spook Who Sat by the Door*, Detroit: Wayne State University Press, 1969, 236.

levels of a society as a people try to figure out, through trial and error, what to make of idled capacities.[5]

It is this change in struggle we have been tracking. The riot is precisely such a reckoning with idled capacities, with the surpluses generated by the production of non-production that characterizes the descent along the arc of accumulation.

Among these surpluses, the most dramatic in its historical development, and the one which most invites a reconsideration of social class, is that part of the population most the subject of the riot: relative surplus population. The logical argument regarding the "progressive production" of this immiserated layer of society, much of which has been touched on already, unfolds over the entirety of the first volume of *Capital* through Chapter 25. It is here we arrive at the summary of the moving contradiction that blooms into both crisis and surplus population, differing aspects of the same process that compels the increasing domination of constant over variable capital, undermining accumulation by expelling labor from the production process: "the working population therefore produces both the accumulation of capital and the means by which it itself is made relatively superfluous; and it does this to an extent which is always increasing."[6] That this completes the book's theoretical argument is signaled by the way Marx then shifts modes entirely, leaping backward for a historical reconstruction of the so-called primitive accumulation and the origin of capital.

Surplus population has multiple strata within it. Perhaps the most significant membrane lies between the reserve army of labor (which remains conceptually within the logic

---

5   Gilmore, *Golden Gulag*, 54.
6   Marx, *Capital*, vol. 1, 783.

of the labor market, driving down wages, moving in and out of the wage with shifts in the supply of and demand for labor), and stagnant surplus population chronically outside the formal wage, or "structurally unemployed," in conventional parlance. For this tranche, the problem of reproduction still presents itself. People finding themselves in this circumstance neither enter into suspended animation nor survive on air. Rather they are pushed into informal economies, often semi- or extralegal, giving them only derivative access to the formal wage. It is this portion of humanity that earns less than subsistence amounts. Informalization can be understood as "ways to organize economic activity with a high return for capital and an excessively low return for labor."[7]

Here we might note the relation of expanded global surplus population and swiftly rising indebtedness over the course of the Long Crisis. It is about this period that Gilles Deleuze dramatically declares, "man is no longer man enclosed, but man in debt." This has been seized on recursively by those anxious to suppose a new economic ontology of debt. Generally forgotten is what Deleuze writes immediately afterward:

> It is true that capitalism has retained as a constant the extreme poverty of three quarters of humanity, too poor for debt, too numerous for confinement: control will not only have to deal with erosions of frontiers but with the explosions within shanty towns or ghettos.[8]

7 Jan Breman, *Outcast Labour in Asia: Circulation and the Informalization of the Workforce at the Bottom of the Economy*, New Delhi: Oxford India Press, 2010, 24. For another systematic treatment of surplus population, see Aaron Benanav, *A Global History of Unemployment since 1949*, London: Verso, forthcoming.

8 Gilles Deleuze, "Postscript on the Societies of Control," *October* 59, Winter 1992, 6–7.

This effectively undermines the strong distinction of Deleuze's initial claim. But it leaves in its place a more incisive recognition, regarding *the unity of the excluded and the indebted*. They are the same global surplus. The explosive growth of the indebted sector is another face of informalization in which finance capital's need to find debtors dovetails with the explosion of populations driven below subsistence wages. The microloan, student loan, and payday loan are parallel instruments, equally unsustainable, in the project to stabilize this growing surplus and somehow preserve them within the circuits of profit.

These are expressions of surplus population within a structural trend of real superfluity. Even as population expands, capital's relative capacity to absorb labor contracts, engendering both a relative and absolute increase in populations "set free" by what we are pleased to call progress, liberated from the burden of work and eventually the burden of life itself. Some scholars have of late noticed that the increase in global struggle draws its force from these populations. Researchers from the Global Social Protest Research Group, working in the tradition of Arrighi and Beverly Silver, detected in the wake of the 2011 wave of uprisings a source that could be located neither in what they call "Marx-type" struggles nor in "Polanyi-type" struggles—based on recent subsumption to the working class and in loss of class privilege, respectively—but instead demanded a new classification: "Protest of the Stagnant Relative Surplus Population."[9]

While attentiveness to traditional class struggles may

9 Sahan Savas Karatasli, Sefika Kumal, Ben Scully, and Smriti Upadhyay, "Class, Crisis, and the 2011 Protest Wave: Cyclical and Secular Trends in Global Labor Unrest," in *Overcoming Global Inequities*, eds. Immanuel Wallerstein, Christopher Chase-Dunn, and Christian Suter, London: Paradigm Publishers, 2015, 192.

have obscured such developments for some until recently, they have long been central to and evident within the Long Crisis. Bremen writes,

> In the 1960s and 1970s, western policymakers viewed the informal economy as a waiting room, or temporary transit zone: newcomers could find their feet there and learn the ways of the urban labor market ... In fact, the trend went in the opposite direction.[10]

The absorption of labor on a global scale concomitant with a renewed ascent along the arc of accumulation does not seem to be in the cards.[11] In the U.S., rising superfluity has been a basic feature of the Long Crisis. The historian Aaron Benanav notes,

> This is especially the case for those formerly employed in the manufacturing sector, which has shed millions of jobs. It is also true for youth who recently entered the labor force for the first time and, above all, for workers of color.

Between 1947 and 1973, the unemployment rate was 4.8 percent on average; after 1973, it rose to 6.5 percent. Since 1973, there has been one exceptional period, 1995–2001, when the unemployment rate returned to its pre-1973 level. Excluding these years, the post-1973 unemployment rate rises to 6.9 percent, or 43 percent above the previous average. This rise is not only due to the fact that unemployment levels have been higher during recessions. Economic

---

10 Breman, *Outcast Labour*, 366.

11 For a thorough assessment of rising surplus population and informalization, see Ibid., 361–8; and Jacques Charmes, "The Informal Economy Worldwide: Trends and Characteristics," *Margin: The Journal of Applied Economic Research* 6: 2, 2012, 103–32.

recoveries are increasingly *jobless recoveries*. Reductions in unemployment have taken longer every decade. Following the 1981 recession, it took 27 months for employment to attain its pre-recession level; following the 1990 recession, 30 months; following the 2000 recession, 46 months. After the 2007 recession, a labor market recovery took 6.3 years.[12]

It is by now impossible to suppose that these phenomena are simply cyclical equilibrations of a labor market that tends toward "full employment" (even as that target has been revised upward). The long-term tendencies are apparent, and the signs we might expect to indicate a secular reversal nowhere to be seen. There are no sails on the horizon. In this context, class might be rethought in ways that exceed the traditional model encountered in the previous chapter, with its relatively static and sociologically positivistic "working class" and accompanying forms of struggle. Given the relative dwindling of this form of labor, Marx must mean something else when, arriving at this conclusion regarding surplus populations, he proposes that "accumulation of capital is therefore multiplication of the proletariat."

Proletarianization and Racialization

The weakness in the static model of the "working class" is not simply in some abstract failure to track capital's restructurings, but in a practical inattention to changes in the subject of struggle. How might we think about riot as a form not just of collective action but of class struggle, when racialization seems to be a core characteristic

---

12 Aaron Benanav, "Precarity Rising," *Viewpoint Magazine*, June 15, 2015.

of *riot prime* in the U.S. and more broadly in the deindustrializing west? It is here that surplus population plays a mediating and deeply explanatory role. Given the ongoing relative and absolute increase of those beyond the productive sectors and beyond the formal economy in general, it may no longer be useful to conceptualize surplus populations as adjuncts to, special cases within, or those excluded from a workforce the image of which we inherit from the era of strong accumulation. We might instead understand *proletariat* not as designating those who labor directly for capital, but in its original sense, a distinction here marked by Gilles Dauvé:

> If one identifies *proletarian* with *factory worker* (or with the manual laborer), or with the poor, one misses what is subversive in the proletarian condition. The proletariat is the negation of this society. It is not the collection of the poor, but of those who are "without reserves," who are nothing, have nothing to lose but their chains, and cannot liberate themselves without destroying the whole social order.[13]

Dauvé presents this as a truth that has been misrecognized, rather than a revision of the category compelled by historical metamorphoses. It is those metamorphoses that matter. The greater the extent to which the historical working class is compelled to affirm capital for its own existence, and the greater the development of "idled capacities," the more we confront the political significance of the expanded proletariat and in particular the role of passive proletarianization, the "dissolving of traditional forms of (re)production."[14]

---

13 Gilles Dauvé, *Eclipse and Re-emergence of the Communist Movement*, Oakland: PM Press, 2015, 47.

14 Thomas Mitschein, Henrique Miranda, and Mariceli Paraense, *Urbanização, selvagem e proletarização passiva na Amazônia: o caso*

This expansion is not, however, neutrally quantitative.

Here we might return to Stuart Hall's clarion formulation, "Race is the modality in which class is lived."[15] This proves even more persuasive and descriptive when envisioning a proletariat that includes surplus populations and thus one that must abandon the sociological model of "worker identity" as an essential component of class belonging. We have already encountered the divergence in rates of wagelessness in Detroit; it is, alas and unsurprisingly, a generalized phenomenon. However, it is not organic. Like chattel slavery itself, it is socially produced. In the span from 1880 to 1910, during a period of labor undersupply, black and white unemployment rates were at parity. The gap opens in the interwar years with "the movement of blacks across industries, especially out of agriculture, and the shift in demand away from the industries in which blacks were employed."[16] The shift toward an industrial and then deindustrializing economy has had, that is to say, a racialized component; since the sixties, black unemployment has been at least double that of white, and in times of crisis this is only intensified. In recent years, black youth unemployment in the cities named in Greenlee's novel has floated near 50 percent; the overall employment profile of these cities is on par with, for comparison, the ongoing disaster of Greece, that crisis without end.

---

de Belém, Belem, 1989, quoted in Mike Davis, *Planet of the Slums*, London: Verso, 2006, 175.

15   Stuart Hall et al., *Policing the Crisis: Mugging, the State, and Law and Order*, London: Macmillan, 1978, 394. While the cited source is collectively authored, this formulation is generally attributed to Hall, in part because it appears in later single-authored works under his name.

16   Robert W. Fairlie and William A. Sundstrom, "The Racial Unemployment Gap in Long-Run Perspective," *The American Economic Review*, 87: 2, May 1997, 307, 309. Note that most data in this study refer to male employment.

Gilmore suggests that we understand transformations of the state apparatus as ways to manage this irremediable surplus, focusing particularly on incarceration:

> In my view, prisons are partial geographical solutions to political economic crises, organized by the state, which is itself in crisis. Crisis means instability that can be fixed only through radical measures, which include developing new relationships and new or renovated institutions out of what already exists. The instability that characterized the end of the golden age of American capitalism provides a key, as we shall see. In the following pages, we shall investigate how certain kinds of people, land, capital, and state capacity became idle—what surplus is—what happened, and why the outcomes are logically explicable but were by no means inevitable.[17]

From this alignment of crisis and surplus, she considers the populations subject to this new regime of state violence, reflecting "on prison demographics, in particular, their exclusive domination of working or workless poor, most of whom are not white." Eventually she concludes:

> The correspondence between regions suffering deep economic restructuring, high rates of unemployment and underemployment among men, and intensive surveillance of youth by the state's criminal justice apparatus present the relative surplus population as the problem for which prison became the state's solution.[18]

The riot, we might note, is the other of incarceration. That is to say, it is a consequence of and response to inexorable

17   Gilmore, *Golden Gulag*, 26–7.
18   Ibid., 15, 113.

and intensifying regimes of exclusion, superfluidity, lack of access to goods, and state surveillance and violence, along with the state's inability to apportion resources toward the social peace. Indeed, these are the specific and local conditions for almost every major rebellion in recent history. If the state's solution to the problem of crisis and surplus is prison—carceral management—the riot is a contest entered directly against this solution—a counterproposal of unmanageability.

An Agenda for Total Disorder

The relation between riot and racialization is among other things an element of the debate regarding who might be the revolutionary subject of the Long Crisis. The significance of surplus populations to this debate arises however not in the early industrializing nations but rather in the decolonizing world, most famously described in Frantz Fanon's *Wretched of the Earth*. He notes that "the formation of a lumpenproletariat is a phenomenon which is governed by its own logic, and neither the overzealousness of missionaries nor decrees from the central authorities can check its growth." Populations are pushed by demographics and expropriation from family lands to the city, where they discover there will be no entrance to the formal economy, and "it is among these masses, in the people of the shanty towns and in the lumpenproletariat that the insurrection will find its urban spearhead," for this cohort "constitutes one of the most spontaneously and radically revolutionary forces of a colonized people."[19]

This shared condition of superfluity, based in dominated populations subjected to ceaseless racialized state

---

19 Frantz Fanon, *The Wretched of the Earth*, New York: Grove Atlantic Press, 2005, 207, 81.

violence, becomes the framework through which Black Power movements achieve mutual recognition with international anticolonial struggles. The coming into maturity of this dispossessed and colonized subject as political agent in the U.S. will be narrated through global antagonisms in a kind of *Bandungsroman*. Groups like Revolutionary Action Movement and the Black Panthers would make careful studies of Fanon among others. It is the logic of the lumpen, of the excluded, that underpins a grasp of colonization as a global process whose terrain of contest is not that of the classical working class. This is fundamental for Newton as he develops his theory of struggle. In keeping with the ambiguity of the situation during the transitions of the sixties, Newton vacillates between seeing the ghettoized black population of the U.S. as the most exploited of a traditional working class, generating superprofits that allow the global projection of the colonial project, and as Fanon's excluded lumpen. "Penned up in the ghettoes of America, surrounded by all his factories and all the physical components of his economic system, we have been made into 'the wretched of the earth,' relegated to the position of spectators," he writes. This situation is ensured by "the occupying army, embodied by the police department," the domestic management of black populations as internal colonization.[20]

Here his argument begins to triangulate with the collapse of the civil rights framework, with its progressive gains that seemed winnable during a period of expansion, and with thinkers like Gilmore regarding the rise of the carceral state as a management of surplus. Capital both sustains and drives colonialism while ensuring the proliferation of surplus populations, in a combined dynamic we

---

20 Newton, *Newton Reader*, 135, 149.

might have called the global division of nonlabor. But it is not capital in a direct sense that disciplines or expropriates surplus populations. Nor is capital able, in the end, to purchase the social peace. The global *classes dangereuses* are united not by their role as producers but by their relation to state violence. In this is to be found the basis of the surplus rebellion and of its form, which must exceed the logic of recognition and negotiation. "Decolonization, which sets out to change the order of the world," declares Fanon, "is clearly an agenda for total disorder."[21]

In light of this we must note that *riot prime* has its origins no more in the marketplace of early modern Europe than in the slave rebellions and anticolonial uprisings of the eighteenth and nineteenth centuries, among those for whom servitude was already enforced by direct and sanctioned violence. Ranajit Guha insists on both the organizational aspect of such struggles and the consequences of effacing it. "Insurgency," he notes, "was a motivated and conscious undertaking on the part of the rural masses." He continues,

> Yet this consciousness seems to have received little notice in the literature on the subject. Historiography has been content to deal with the peasant rebel merely as an empirical person or member of a class, but not as an entity whose will and reason constituted a praxis called rebellion. The omission is dyed into most narratives by metaphors assimilating peasant revolts to natural phenomena: they break out like thunderstorms, heave like earthquakes, infect like epidemics.[22]

21 Fanon, *Wretched*, 3.
22 Ranajit Guha, "The Prose of Counter-Insurgency," in *Selected Subaltern Studies*, eds. Ranajit Guha and Gayatri Chakravorty Spivak, Oxford: Oxford University Press, 1988, 46.

The insight enters into the familiar debate between agency and determination. If it limits itself to one side of the dialectical pairing, that is surely in an effort to disclose the pernicious rhetorical effects of the opposite one-sidedness and its supposed objectivity. Guha captures eloquently an effect noted earlier, in which the purported spontaneity of such rebellions becomes an ideological opportunity to treat rebels as reflexive and natural, lacking in rationality, unsovereign, socially determined but not determining, not fully human—which in turn allows the ongoing racialization of riot's participants, and implicit justification for racialized domination. To riot is to fail the measure of the human. To fail to be the subject.

One can see examples of this antagonistic debate over proper subjects at the very outset of the Long Crisis. In 1972, Alain Badiou dismisses with no little sarcasm "the brilliant novelty of the dissident marginal masses," a dismissal earned through their association with disorder (under the usual theoretical rubrics of flux and free play and so forth), in favor of Marx and Engels's "finally coherent systematization of the revolutionary practices of their time."[23] Of the many proponents of this view, Badiou is particularly suggestive for his later shifts in sympathy to the side of the "rabble," in his *Rebirth of History* (in which he sympathetically adopts the racially coded term "*racaille*" for his protagonists, the word for "rabble" weaponized by then Minister of the Interior Sarkozy against the French rioters of 2005). It is an incomplete shift, however: for Badiou's "generic communism," order is still the order of the day, although now under the rubric of the Idea rather than the

---

23 Alain Badiou, *Théorie de la contradiction*, Paris: Librairie François Maspero, 1972, 72. Translated by Eleanor Kaufman in "The Desire Called Mao: Badiou and the Legacy of Libidinal Economy," *Postmodern Culture* 18: 1, September 2007.

Party. Nonetheless, his traverse does register a more thoroughgoing change in the material basis for understandng these actors that dissolves any antinomy between the "dissident marginal masses" and a view of how revolutionary possibilities might unfold.

This is the vital content of the recomposition of class at a global level. Guha's insistence on the conscious and reasoned aspect, the revolutionary subjectivity, of seemingly spontaneous uprisings in what has sometimes been called the "periphery" exemplifies one retort to those who would dismiss such struggles. Alone, it remains partial. Fanon's account of the remorseless arrival of surplus populations onto the political stage, and their intransigent relation to certain forms of collective action, is its necessary complement. The trajectory he traces has only intensified as "the cities have become a dumping ground for a surplus population working in unskilled, unprotected and low-wage informal service industries and trade."[24] The scope of this development is compassed in Mike Davis's *Planet of Slums*, an overwhelming summary of global surplus populations. One aspect of this dynamic is the certainty that these developments will make their way ever more dramatically to the deindustrializing core as racialized superfluity progresses.

There has been, then, a sort of double arrival of riot to the deindustrializing west. Or, rather, of the conditions in which the struggles that will be called riots are inevitable. It has come down from the export and marketplace riots of the seventeenth and eighteenth centuries, and come inward from periphery to core. The double motion is a convergence of colonialist and capitalist logics, their disorders coming home to roost.

---

24   United Nations Human Settlements Program, *The Challenge of Slums: Global Reports on Human Settlements*, 2003, London: Routledge, 2003, 40.

The Public Riot

Early on we encountered the first weakness in the category "race riot": the ambiguity of "race" itself. Gilmore, along with many other scholars, argues that race has no autonomous existence. But neither is it a figment. Rather, it is produced through a process that she calls "racism" and which we have been calling "racialization," which she defines as "the state-sanctioned or extralegal production and exploitation of group-differentiated vulnerability to premature death."[25] Chris Chen argues for focusing not on "race" but on racial ascription, the structural processes though which race is produced, as distinct "from voluntary acts of cultural identification—and from a range of responses to racial rule from flight to armed revolt."[26] Concurring with the larger argument, we would, however, suggest that preexisting ideological assignments of meaning (and nonmeaning) to uprisings and riots take part in such ascription. The riot, for all its systematically produced inevitability, is one of the moments of vulnerability of which Gilmore speaks; it is the form of struggle given to surplus populations, already racialized. To enter into riot is to be in the category of persons whose location in the social structure compels them to some forms of collective action rather than others. Thus we might finally argue that the term "race riot" has an inverted sense: not that of race as cause of riot, but of riot as part of the ongoing process of racialization. It is not that race makes riots but that riots make race.

This formulation must return us once more to the discovery that "race is the modality in which class is lived." The phrase has become so well known that it has evaded

---

25   Gilmore, *Golden Gulag*, 28.
26   Chen, "Limit Point," 205.

its context. It turns out to be a claim about, among other things, riots. In a generally overlooked earlier passage of the same coauthored text, we find a more expansive formulation grounding the phrase in concrete struggles. "It is in the modality of race that those whom the structures systematically exploit, exclude and subordinate discover themselves as an exploited, excluded and subordinated class. Thus it is primarily in and through the modality of race that resistance, opposition and rebellion *first* expresses itself."[27]

The "*first*" is significant. It implies that the confrontational encounters open eventually onto other modalities—onto class, we conclude, given the later epigrammatic formulation. At the same time, "modality" seeks to overcome the hierarchy of appearance and essence, wherein what might appear to be an experience of race is later revealed as the truth of class. Rather, there is a continuity and a commingling. Here we must recall that Hall's formula originally centers itself on blackness, and difficulties arise when this is casually adduced to race more broadly. In the U.S. and U.K., in differing ways, a historical antiblackness has constituted hierarchies of racialization such that poor black populations approach absolute exposure to superfluity and to state violence. Along this hierarchy, we find a shifting interplay of exploitation and exclusion, impersonal dominations and directly violent management. The logic of a structurally racialized surplus informing a new proletariat traverses the seeming antinomy of race and class to reveal racialization as both feature and engine of class recomposition.

At the same time, the category of surplus allows for a flexible and even capacious means of assessing ongoing transformations. Surplus is not synonymous with race;

---

27 Hall et al., *Crisis*, 347 (emphasis in original).

neither is it easily extricable from it. We are in the midst of an ongoing exodus to the overdeveloped world driven by geopolitical volatility and by capital's incapacity to absorb adequate labor in emerging regions of the world-system—a diaspora inseparable from expanding superfluity. This cannot help but put pressure on protocols of racialization as well, on the forms and framings of exclusion. In light of this contemporary emergence of surplus populations and of the politics of surplus we might now advance from the previous suggestion of riot as a modality of race to an expanded proposition: *riot is the modality through which surplus is lived.*

To say this is to say that *circulation prime* is the era of *riot prime,* and not simply in the sense that it features an increase in riot events both absolute and relative to strikes. *Riot prime* is the condition in which surplus life *is* riot, is the subject of politics and the object of ongoing state violence. Within the social reorganization of the Long Crisis, the public of surplus is treated as riot at all times—incipient, in progress, in exhaustion—not out of error but out of recognition. As the philosopher Nina Power writes in her contradictory inventory "Thirty-One Theses on the Problem of the Public," "The public has never existed"—but also, "the public does not always coincide with the nothing it is supposed to be." Surplus is nothing and must be everything. Thus Thesis 31: "The public is a slow-moving riot."[28]

Power also notes that "the police are the public and the public is the police." The ambiguity arises no doubt from the phrase's source with Robert Peel, founder of modern policing in the UK, and with his vision of policing as

---

28 Nina Power, "Thirty-One Theses on the Problem of the Public," *Objective Considerations of Contemporary Phenomena,* MOTINTERNATIONAL, 2014.

expression of a more general social will rather than being a force imposed from without. A noble thought no doubt. The desultory truth of this sense lies in the way the public, as a population made civic, takes up a kind of liberal self-policing, which is always passively present and often comes forward during active riots as freedom-loving citizens hurry to discipline their compeers with pleas for an ethical pacifism that, if at first ignored, are repeated with the accompanying threat that a uniformed officer will be summoned to help with the agitator's emancipation. The riot in this regard bears its police within itself.

This is doubly true, for another possible sense, encountered earlier, lies in the integration of the state's police function with *riot prime*. Given the ways that state violence now exists in the place of the economy, the public of surplus exists in an economy of state violence. But this acts as a limit. Such ongoing exposure provides a unity and self-recognition, and thus cannot be easily done away with. This is a conundrum for the public of surplus, for *riot prime*, one that becomes apparent when open riot bursts forth:

> The police, in this sense, are not an external force of order applied by the state to an already rioting mass, but an integral part of the riot: not only its standard component spark-plug, acting via the usual death, at police hands, of some young black man, but also the necessary ongoing partner of the rioting crowd from whom the space must be liberated if this liberation is to mean anything at all; who must be attacked as an enemy if the crowd is to be unified in anything; who must be forced to *recognize* the agency of a habitually subjected group.[29]

---

29 "A Rising Tide Lifts All Boats," *Endnotes* 3, 2013, 98.

One cannot help encountering in this relationship the Hegelian recognition scene, the police-riot dialectic so characteristic of *riot prime*. Immediately we recall Fanon's transposing of the same scene to the colonial situation—as well as Susan Buck-Morss's contention that Hegel drew on the anticolonial struggle of Haiti for his original formulation, so that Fanon's rendering is less a transposition than the completion of a circuit.[30] The struggle for decolonization, in Fanon's telling, must transcend recognition, given that the colonized can be absorbed neither into the state as free citizens nor into the economy as free labor. Thus it must come down to "quite simply the substitution of one 'species' of mankind for another. The substitution is unconditional, absolute, total, and seamless."[31]

We must be clear that the situation of the Long Crisis in the deindustrializing nations is not assimilable to the scene of anticolonial struggle. Neither, as noted above, is it unrelated to it. The conceptual separations of core and periphery, first and third worlds, and so on have less purchase than ever. The juncture, as has been suggested, is in the rising presence of a population whose labor can never be objectified. Redistribution is off the table as the haves cling ever more implacably to the world-system's dwindling wealth, concentrating it still further. The structurally excluded gather in the streets and the square, in the holding areas and outer rings of the gleaming, dying cities. *We are the crisis.* Historically, the regimes of accumulation in the U.K. and U.S. have found ways to absorb these populations, to provide a route to their self-reproduction that is also the reproduction of capital. Now the question of proletarian reproduction increasingly looks beyond the wage.

30 Susan Buck-Morss, "Hegel and Haiti," *Critical Inquiry* 26: 4, Summer 2000, 821–65.

31 Fanon, *Wretched*, 1.

Neither, however, can the subjects of *riot prime* imagine meaningful subsistence in the marketplace, in the manner of the previous era of riot. The separation of production and exchange and the presence of the police is the absence of that possibility. The great class recomposition and the abstraction of the economy are one and the same. Price-setting even in its contemporary form proves the most transient of palliatives. The public whose modality is riot must eventually encounter the need to pursue reproduction not just beyond the wage but beyond the marketplace.

It is in this regard that the riot is the sign of a situation that must in the end absolutize itself. Not because of some wild and affective nature of riot, though those who have had such experiences know that this is an astonishing force, but because of the still unfolding and still deteriorating situation in which it finds itself. *Riot prime* is not a demand but a civil war.

We have, then, something like a last contradiction. On the one hand, the riot must absolutize itself, move toward a self-reproduction beyond wage and market, toward the social arrangement that we define as the commune, always a civil war. On the other hand, the riot is entangled both internally and externally with the police function that seems a blockage to any such absolutization. This contradiction offers some ways to think about the riots, rebellions, and uprisings of the years since the global market collapse of 2008—the historical particulars they embody, the failures they bear, the future they suggest.

Lacking the scope of surveys, models will have to do. Two examples will be particularly suggestive in considering the current situation of *riot prime* in the overdeveloped world. Two landscapes, then, the square and the street. Just as the port and the factory were the place of riot and strike respectively, these are the natural homes of *riot prime*.

They are places of circulation, the circulation of bodies and goods. They at once valorize the logic of circulation struggles and display this dynamic's incomplete historical development. One landscape is the 2011 series of plaza occupations known as Occupy, the U.S. iteration of the international movement of the squares. The other is the 2014 riots, first local and then national, following, respectively, the murder of Michael Brown in Ferguson, Missouri, and the decision not to indict his killer, the police office Darren Wilson. When those riots escape from their suburb, they leap to twenty cities, including each locale named in the passage from *The Spook Who Sat by the Door*.

CHAPTER 9

Riot Now: Square, Street, Commune

The riot, the blockade, the barricade, the occupation. The commune. These are what we will see in the next five, fifteen, forty years. The list is not new. It has become a kind of common sense among a few groups that identify themselves with the end of the program. The goal here is not to reiterate the items, nor simply to explicate why they are more likely to be effective now than they were at some previous moment. This is surely the case. This book's argument, nonetheless, is not that circulation struggles name the correct approach for "blocking capital" (or however some might phrase it) so as to bring it to heel. Circulation is value in motion toward realization; it is also a regime of social organization within capital, interlocking with production in a shifting relation whose disequilibrium appears as crisis. We have tried to set forth the theoretical and historical bases for "circumstances existing already, given and transmitted from the past," for why within these circumstances further circulation struggles are inevitable, and how a fuller understanding of this conceptual framework and material history might mediate between *is* and *ought*. This will require grappling with the limits to the most recent wave of struggles, while at the same time trying to draw forth the practical kernel, as it were, from which forthcoming struggles are certain to bloom.

The Square and Class Alliance

The classical Greek *agora* is both marketplace and public assembly, a double character that persists in increasingly ghostly fashion into the first era of riots. The return of *riot prime* to the square recalls the marketplace struggles of the first era of riot, recalls those struggles' social claim conducted through the economy. It cannot but do so. At the same time, it demonstrates the impossibility of such a return.

When the varied iterations of the "movement of the squares" that oriented global struggle in 2010–11 arise in the agora, they present in many regards a clear demonstration of this book's argument. They go directly to the exemplary site of circulation. Their basis in surplus populations is manifest. One might consider the precipitation of the Arab Spring by the self-immolation of Mohamed Bouazizi, one of a rising mass of Tunisians driven into the informal economy and then subjected to ceaseless harassment by the police. Such a precipitation depends on the exceptional nature of the episode, its paroxysm of immiseration. But it depends simultaneously on the paradigmatic nature of Bouazizi's situation, as one among the many rendered surplus by political-economic transformations, unabsorbable, futureless, pitched up in the public spaces of the cities.

And yet the location of *riot prime* in the modern square is a signal of its confinement to the space of politics. This is more or less the transcendental problem of 2011. Realized capitalism rests on the separation of the political and the economic, the authority of the people able to be conceptualized independently from the supposedly technocratic problems of resource creation and distribution. This separation is expressed in the distance between our leading riotologies, encountered earlier: on the one hand, Badiou's politics of the idea, and on the other, the mechanical economism of the New England Complex Systems Institute and others. The population of *riot prime*, we might now recognize, achieves a historical order not through a shared idea, not by the deadly fluctuations of food prices, but corresponding to an underlying political-economic unity, a material reorganization of society, which provides them a shared set of problems and a shared arena in which to confront them.

The snares of the political are many. The Occupy encampments' requirement of violent repression and accompanying outrage in order to expand parallels its broader orientation toward the state and its institutions. Another snare is seen in the long riot of the Greek crisis: its *antikristos* of antagonists and police, unremitting since 2008, precedes and premises the encampment in Athens' Syntagma Square and the repetitive attacks on the Parliament building. Arguably the most distressing example of the political snare is the discovery that the seeming public coups of the Arab Spring give forth formalist revolutions of fatal incompleteness. *The people want the fall of the regime.* "But this antagonism is in fact endless, circular," as some have noted. "Nothing can make this circularity more plain than the departure of Mohamed Morsi, 30 months after Hosni Mubarak's fall, one year and a week after his own election. It turns out that it was *not* the fall of the regime the people wanted, was not democracy in some abstract sense."[1] Despite the rehabilitation projects undertaken by various philosophers, democracy remains the contrary of absolutization. "If we begin with the state, we end with the

---

[1] Research and Destroy, "The Wreck of the Plaza," June 14, 2014, researchanddestroy.wordpress.com. This article previously appeared under the suggestive title "Plaza-Riot-Commune."

state," remarks Kristin Ross, arguing that to narrate the nativity of the Paris Commune as a confrontation between a population and its government is to limit our understanding of the event to one of a contest for control over a state that remains the state.[2] This is a limit for both theory and practice, not least for our grasp of all the ways that the modern state evolves from and requires the structures of capital.

This issueless democratic urge will be nowhere more present than in the U.S., where deliberation becomes an end in and of itself. The practical goals of Occupy Wall Street (OWS) are swiftly bracketed. Originally it declares its intent (somewhat implausibly) to block the stock exchange, to interrupt the virtualized whooshing of financial capital itself. Pushed swiftly into the square it would make famous, enclosed by barricades and police, it streams periodically into the streets or onto the Brooklyn Bridge. Its other stated purpose is to develop a single demand against the financial oligarchy understood to have delivered the financial crisis, and against the austerity politics delivered in turn. It becomes clear quickly if tacitly that any specific demand will fracture the fragile gathering. And so the camp becomes "its own demand," at once a call for recognition of the lived misery of austerity and an imagined prefiguration of future self-management. It is telling that the most famous innovation of OWS will be the "human microphone," a way of communicating.

Occupy Oakland will share generic similarities with OWS, and no shortage of deliberation. Its differences will be more telling. The most militant of the encampments, it bodies forth the idea of riot as modality, not only because it regularly leaps into the city streets and into open riot.

2   Kristin Ross, *Communal Luxury: The Political Imaginary of the Paris Commune*, Verso: London, 2015, 14.

Understood according to the intense condensation of wealth, gentrification, and rising inequality peculiar (but not unique) to Oakland and the Bay Area, the Occupy Oakland's regular destruction of property is a kind of price-setting: an attempt to depress climbing property values by undermining bourgeois standards of habitability. At the same time, it goes directly to the economy. Twice the occupiers close the vast Port of Oakland (both times in uncomfortable collaboration with the longshore and warehouse union), once within an attempted general strike—the first in the United States since 1946. Alongside these classic circulation struggles, it can be no surprise that Occupy Oakland centered on a communal kitchen, signaling the centrality of surplus population to the encampment.

Despite its role within the national web of encampments in autumn 2011, the formation of Occupy Oakland should be equally registered in the light of other histories. One of these is the "double riot," a misrecognized commonplace at a systemic level. In France, the 2005 riots leap from banlieue to banlieue, particularly those with heavily informalized and immigrant populations, following the deaths of Zyed Benna and Bouna Traoré while fleeing the police; in 2006, the so-called CPE riots respond to attempts to restructure youth labor markets and feature university occupations. The pattern repeats in the U.K. in reverse order: first the 2010 student struggles, including both university occupations and the sacking of Tory headquarters; then the Tottenham riots of 2011, after the killing of Mark Duggan. In Oakland, riots at the outset of 2009 follow the police murder of Oscar Grant; 2009–10 sees a series of university occupations drawing militarized repression across California (and the nation), but centered in neighboring Berkeley.

The shape of the double riot is clear enough. One riot arises from youth discovering that the routes that once promised a minimally secure formal integration into the economy are now foreclosed. The other arises from racialized surplus populations and the violent state management thereof. The holders of empty promissory notes, and the holders of nothing at all. When this contemporary pairing is recognized, the two sides are purported to be in opposition, the abjection of one betraying the relative privilege of this other. This is itself a one-sided understanding of crisis and its populations, of the modes and temporalities through which exclusion unfolds. The task is not to discover new sociological categories that can supersede the stale classifications of a previous era, replacing one reified set of actors with another. Rather, it is to bring forward the real movement within which these social categories develop, change, elaborate themselves internally and in relation to other social forces. The Oakland encampment, which briefly named itself the Oakland Commune, might be understood as an impossible attempt to synthesize the two constituencies of the double riot—and as a lived instance of these populations' increasingly shared terrain of struggle, their unfinished motion toward each other.

The camp's composition was its strength and weakness: the basis of its militancy and the terms of its unsustainable class alliance between the excluded and foreclosed. The camp composition captures "a central contradiction embedded in contemporary manifestations of tent city ... between the abjection of the refugee camp and the activism of the political camp" as Sasha X names matters.[3] This description, however, misses the ongoing subsumption of "the political camp" within political-economic conditions.

---

3   Sasha X, "Occupy Nothing: Utopia, History, and the Common Abject," *Mediations* 28: 1, Fall 2014, 62.

It would be equally accurate to describe Occupy Oakland as an instance of incomplete proletarianization. In its moment it is not yet quite possible to unify the double riot in a single camp. This manifests most clearly in the contradiction between ideology and practice. The dominant discourse of Occupy—"we are the 99 percent," and so deserving of an equivalent share of social wealth and class power—is unable to represent those whose lives are already beyond the promises of institutional betterment and redistributive politics. There is little recognition within that formulation of the material relation between the Occupy movement and the planet of slums, even as that planet increasingly features places like Oakland. At the same time, however, Oakland's forms of struggle (riot, general strike, port shutdown) comport more clearly with the politics of surplus populations, politics without program.

Such politics, tending toward absolutization, would not go unopposed. Those still able to project, from within their social circumstance, an image of redistribution and restoration to some previous moment of social equilibrium (always resembling the dispensation of the Long Boom and a nostalgic Keynesianism) were often willing to enforce this view via passive and active collaboration with police. This would prove an obstruction equal to the police themselves.

For all that, the encampment was singular. Certainly it stood out from the national map of Occupy encampments: all black blocs and bad blood, portions of it engaging a qualitatively different politics, confronting the austerity state as antagonist rather than betrayed partner, a Society of Enemies for whom fighting the police was less a goal than an inevitability of position. It is more continuous with an international narrative, a red thread that winds from the banlieue riots to all tomorrow's tear gas parties. The ongoing alliance or indistinction between encampments of surplus population and other political aggregates that cannot be appropriated to a partnership with the state is a basic characteristic of *riot prime*—and one certain to expand and intensify as it continues to mutate along with increasing production of nonproduction and global political volatility.

The Street and the Rift

The logic of circulation struggles has seen no more spectacular instance than that of November 24–25, 2014, when riot spread to city after city from a suburb of St. Louis, following a moment of intolerable violence, of the fatal management of racialized populations, beginning in the way riots begin in the age of *riot prime*, not out of nowhere but out of everywhere. The place of this riot is the street, the street where Michael Brown was murdered, the street where people gathered to await the news that his killer would not be indicted, the street where people met up afterward. The street where anti-police violence cleared space for the looting of commercial venues, and allowed for evasions toward other targets. And eventually the freeways, on a continental scale, shutting down junction after spur throughout the Interstate Highway System, the built landscape of circulation, once the largest public works project known to history. And yet this should not be reduced to spectacle, to representation. The blocking of traffic, the interruption of circulation as an immediate and concrete project, registered nothing so much as the unquenchable desire to *make it all stop*. The freeways and thoroughfares were the closest matter to hand of *it all*, of the antihuman totalization and thingification of the world.

The matching scenes from around the nation convey an uncanny sense of coordination, of organization without an organization. The riots would be driven to national expansion not just by the impunity of the police officer but by a series of intervening killings across the country, cop on person, links on an endless chain. Even more remarkable and more suggestive than these riots' spatial leap, however, is their initial duration. It is in this that the true novelty of Ferguson lies.

After Michael Brown was shot to death by Darren Wilson, the local riots began almost immediately and lasted for more than two weeks. The measuring of riot is an inexact science; nonetheless, this sequence would seem to have outlasted any of the similar cases already discussed, from Detroit, Newark, and Chicago through to the present. Anyone who has been to Ferguson will recognize how extraordinary is this fact. A small incorporated city just north of St. Louis, its population is about 20,000, down from a peak of 30,000 around 1970 before deindustrialization had its way. There is not a fortnight's worth of things to burn. There is no plaza to be occupied, but the complicity between street and square persists. On the commercial strip of West Florissant Avenue, epicenter of the riots, people burned down the QuikTrip market and used the lot as their plaza until it was sealed off by the state.

The racial transformation of the city has been striking even as it has followed an increasingly common course, going from about three-quarters white and one-quarter black in 1990 to nearly the inverse by 2010. The traditional U.S. structure of white flight that once rendered inner cities holding areas for surplus population has mutated to resemble the European and global model of banlieues and bidonvilles that gather surplus populations in rings around cities.

Phil A. Neel offers a clear account of how these demographic shifts and the geography of the attenuated landscape provide the terms for the "suburban riot," whose locus classicus is in the decentralized and demandless uprising of Los Angeles in 1992.[4] Neel locates an additional coordinate toward explaining the difficulty of containing the riot: the absence of a mediating class of black leaders dedicated to order in the name of community. This is a telling expression of what is in truth a much larger structural shift.

It is a nearly universal convention of *riot prime*, of the rebellion, the uprising, that shortly after it bursts forth and experiences a victory either substantial or apparent, it divides into two impulses. These are sometimes openly antagonistic, sometimes overlapping and colluding. The first impulse is toward a kind of populism, an attempt to swell the ranks by mobilizing public sympathies, using to its advantage media coverage and other discursive apparatuses. It is drawn ineluctably toward some version of respectability politics and generally toward the moral suasion of passive civil disobedience and nonviolence in general. It intends to develop a political force, sway opinion, win concessions. Eventually it will be drawn without fail into the electoral arena, subordinated as plank or caucus of party politics. If this political fraction is early on called upon to justify the disorder of riot, it takes up the affirmation of Martin Luther King Jr. that "a riot is the language of the unheard." This has an immediate appeal; it would be difficult not to hear in any uprising the wail of the immiserated. And yet it presents an underexamined symptomology, presupposing that the inchoate cry of riot must in truth have some as yet undeciphered meaning beyond itself, and moreover that this meaning-making is its primary aspect—those other unfortunate aspects one sees on the news are disavowed in the universal humanist

4 Phil A. Neel, "New Ghettos Burning," August 17, 2014, ultra-com.org.

appeal to recognize the suffering of the other and even forgive the excesses in its expression. Within this understanding, even the demandless riot is transcoded into *being itself a demand*, something that could be satisfied by the current order if it could just be understood. Negotiation becomes a transhistorical truth.

The second impulse finds in the riot something beyond or before communication. It turns less toward a polity than toward practicalities, turns toward the material in both low and high senses. These practicalities might include looting, controlling space, eroding the power of the police, rendering an area unwelcoming to intruders, and destroying property understood to constitute the rioters' exclusion from the world they see always before them and which they may not enter.

This division is as old as riot itself and is not cleanedged. There are practical aspects to discursive acts, and conversely the broken window or burned shop is inevitably a kind of communication. Nonetheless the rift is evident, socially lived by participants, and repeated largely without fail. This would also prove the case in Ferguson, where each night of the riots would feature both peaceful marches that largely followed police prescriptions, and less orderly actions that included arson and firing on police officers. While the factions worked in collaboration during the first few days, or perhaps had not yet fully formed, they came to be increasingly at odds, particularly after a large number of national clergy arrived in Ferguson to amplify what they took to be the lessons of Dr. King.

But it is here that a historical shift lurches into view, one of primary importance. Since the Civil Rights movement (and before it the "first generation" of the feminist movement), the side of legal frameworks, moral suasion, and respectability politics has effectively hegemonized the debate fairly swiftly after each uprising. This has been the case in no small part because said approach could offer real, if limited, gains. Such outcomes no longer seem plausible. The success of the discursive strategy was premised upon a certain degree of social wealth, taut labor markets, a continuity of profit worth preserving even if it meant relative sacrifices for capital.

One could perhaps imagine demands in the present that would, if met, alter in substance the circumstances of the excluded. But the swelling ranks of the excluded is the same fact as the inability to meet such demands—the two faces of crisis. Just as the U.S. can no longer deliver accumulation at a global level, and thus must order the world-system by coercion rather than consent, the state can no longer provide the kinds of concessions won by the Civil Rights movement, can no longer purchase the social peace. It is all sticks and no carrots. The Baltimore riots following the murder of Freddie Gray in 2015, whose duration and intensity would be met by the National Guard and a nine-day state of emergency, only affirm this situation.

Because of this, the rift can no longer be so easily closed. The prolongation of the riots and of their fury is doubtless a measure of social pressures building around racialized policing and around the immanent violence applied to the management of surplus populations in general. It is also a measure of the fading appeal of moderation and optimistic compliance. This approach still retains some charisma, as the ongoing institutionalization of the Ferguson and Baltimore uprisings within the containment of Non-Governmental Organizations attests. At the same time, the argument that the bottomless violence and subordination is structural, and cannot be resolved either practically or theoretically through redistributive participation, grows ever harder to refute.

Barring unforeseeable changes in underlying social organization, the rift will grow wider and stay open longer. This is how the drive toward absolutization appears at a practical level. If we understand each like instance as a rift of increasing duration, the number of rifts open at any given time will increase as well. It is foreseeable that a cascading series of them—initially but not exclusively oriented by racialized struggles—will succeed in preserving their own existences while drawing forth other struggles to take their main chance against a spreading disorder, a disorder that now seems to belong not to riot but to the state, to what had previously been itself a violent order. Against this great disorder, a necessary self-organization, survival in a different key. One need not think this likely to think it more likely than a renewed socialist program, even one given new trappings for a purportedly new economy.

Commune and Catastrophe

If the square and the street have been the two places of *riot prime*, they both open onto the commune. The commune, however, is not a place in that sense, not a "territorial agglomeration," as Kropotkin expressed it.[5] Its history has been to escape that designation, even while specific instances take on the names of their sites. One might say it is instead a social relation, a political form, an event. It has been called all of these. We have also suggested that it is a tactic, understandable within this book's development of Tilly's repertoires of collective action. This may seem a curious holding for such a sustained and elaborate endeavor as the commune. A last diversion, then, to make sense of such a claim, and gather it into something else altogether.

---

5   Ross, *Communal Luxury*, 123–4.

Bruno Bosteels, in dislocating the commune from the all-encompassing exemplarity of Paris, provides a pivotal insight. In his study of what historian Adolfo Gilly named the Morelos Commune (peaking in 1914–15), he concedes,

At the level of organizational forms of appearance, anarchism is accused of favoring spontaneous uprisings and attacks as part of its ideology of direct action, to which only a socialist class-consciousness, aimed at the seizure of state power, is said to lend the necessary organization of an enduring political movement.[6]

This antinomy, with its already ideological conjoining of political identification and forms of action, is precisely what the commune dissolves: "However, there is one political form in which anarchists and socialists—even in Mexico—seem able to find common ground: the form of the commune."[7] This multiplicity of the commune is noted by Marx about Paris, from which he abstracts a more univocal lesson:

Its true secret was this. It was essentially a working-class government, the product of the struggle of the producing against the appropriating class, the political form at last discovered under which to work out the economic emancipation of labor.[8]

This conclusion is ambiguous if one takes Morelos as a case study against Paris, given its provisional continuity of

---

6 Bruno Bosteels, "The Mexican Commune," in *Communism in the Twenty-First Century*, vol. 2, ed. Shannon Brincat, Santa Barbara: Praeger, 2014, 168.

7 Ibid.

8 Karl Marx and V. I. Lenin, *The Civil War in France: The Paris Commune*, New York: International Publishers, 1968, 60.

peasant and worker, agrarian reform alongside anticapitalist struggles in the swiftly industrializing sugar mills (an
ambiguity Bosteels extends throughout the subterranean
history of the "Mexican Commune," through the Zapatista
uprising of 1994 and the Oaxaca Commune of 2006). That
is to say, from this perspective it does not seem at all clear
that the compositional secret of the commune is a singular
"working-class government" so much as the communality
of various social fractions.

And this is exactly the point. Within the transformations
of the present, the form of the commune is unthinkable
without the modulation from traditional working class to
an expanded proletariat. That is to say, it is not oriented by
productive laborers, but rather by the heterogeneous population of those without reserves. Like the riot, the commune
may feature workers but not necessarily as workers. Ross
argues that the commune is defined in part by the fullness
of its relation.

What the commune as political and social medium offered
that the factory did not was a broader social scope—one
that included women, children, the peasantry, the aged, the
unemployed. It comprised not merely the realm of production but both production and consumption.[9]

This is at first a curious claim, as it is capitalism itself that
is founded on the interlocking circuits of production and
consumption, a pairing that has provided us with the two
ur-forms of modern struggle: strike and riot, wage- and price-
setting. The implication must be that the commune offers
production and consumption of needs (and of pleasures!—
"communal luxuries," as Ross has it) beyond the measures

---

9 Ross, *Communal Luxury*, 112.

of capital. Which is to say, beyond wage and price. Just so, in theory. Communism in the present, no longer able to be conflated with worker command over production and distribution in the socialist mode, is the breaking of the index between one's labor input and one's access to necessities —the twin social activities regulated by wage and price respectively. It may preserve production and consumption in a general sense. But it does away with the mediations that bind production to consumption. Only then are the compulsions of value that organize social relations broken.

But, lurking in the shadows cast by the abstract light of the ideal, there is equally a practical and concrete sense of this recognition that the commune is beyond capitalist production and consumption. If we turn at the last moment to material histories, it is because we set out from nowhere else. Neither the Paris nor Morelos communes can be understood independently from the social catastrophes— the *overturnings*—that preceded them.[10] The commune appears beyond wage and price because those struggles cease to be possible in any practical sense, because human reproduction in that moment is not to be found in either the workplace or the marketplace. To the degree that the commune is a historical opening, it is as well a foreclosure, and this foreclosure is inseparable from its working existence. As Marx reminds us, "The great social measure of the Commune was its own working existence."[11]

The commune, then, has a continuity with the riot. It presupposes the impossibility of wage-setting as a means

---

10   For a survey of the political-economic conditions of Morelos in advance of the Commune, see Paul Hart, *Bitter Harvest: The Social Transformation of Morelos, Mexico, and the Origins of the Zapatista Revolution, 1840–1910*, Albuquerque: University of New Mexico, 2005, 149, 191–2.

11   Marx, *Civil War*, 65.

to secure any manner of emancipation. It is likely to be inaugurated, like many struggles in the first era of riots, by those for whom the question of reproduction beyond the wage has long been posed—those who have been socially forged as the bearers of that crisis. "The women were the first to act," we are reminded by Lissagaray about the Paris Commune, "hardened by the siege—they had had a double ration of misery."[12] That siege which is gender has never ended.

At the same time, the commune also ruptures from the riot's basis in price-setting, because provisioning toward subsistence is no longer to be found in such action. It is beyond strike and riot both. In such a situation, the commune emerges not as an "event" but as a tactic of social reproduction. It is critical to understand the commune first as a tactic, as *a practice to which theory is adequate.* Beyond strike and riot, what distinguishes the problems and possibilities of reproduction from those of production and consumption is this: the commune is a tactic that is also a form of life.

The coming communes will develop where both production and circulation struggles have exhausted themselves. The coming communes are likely to emerge first not in walled cities or in communities of retreat, but in open cities where those excluded from the formal economy and left adrift in circulation now stand watch over the failure of the market to provide their needs. The *glacis* around Thiers's Wall is now the *Boulevard Periphérique*; surplus population gathers now on the ring roads around Lima, Dhaka, and Dar es Salaam. But not just there.

Things fall apart, core and periphery cannot hold. We turn round and round in the night and are consumed by

---

12 Prosper-Olivier Lissagaray, *History of the Paris Commune of 1871*, trans. Eleanor Marx Aveling, London: Verso, 2012, 65.

fire. Perhaps the Long Crisis of capital may reverse; it is a dangerous wager on either side. Within the persistence of crisis, however, the reproduction of capital through the circuit of production and circulation—wage and market—appears increasingly not as possibility for, but limit to, proletarian reproduction. A dead and burning circuit. Here riot returns late and appears early, both too much and too little. The commune is nothing but the name for the attempt to overcome this limit, a peculiar catastrophe still to come.

On the Typeface

This book is set in Sabon, a narrow Garamond-style book face designed in 1968 by the German typographer Jan Tschichold. Tschichold had been a leading voice of sans-serif modernist typography, particularly after the publication of his *Die neue Typographie* in 1928. As a result, the Nazis charged him with "cultural Bolshevism" and forced him to flee Germany for Switzerland.

Tschichold soon renounced modernism—comparing its stringent tenets to the "teachings of National Socialism and fascism"—and extolled the qualities of classical typography, exemplified in his design for Sabon, which he based on the Romain S. Augustin de Garamond in the 1592 Egenolff-Berner specimen sheet.

Sabon is named after the sixteenth-century French typefounder Jacques Sabon, a pupil of Claude Garamond and proprietor of the Egenolff foundry.

Index

Index

surplus population, 26–7,
163, 180, 186; of wageless
life, 27
reproduction: and capital,
45, 46, 172, 192; and
circulation, 47, 192; and
double moulinet, 45; and
economic reorganization,
28; from eighteenth to
nineteenth centuries, 15; of
labor power, 45, 172; and
looting, 29; and markets,
51, 123, 151, 192; and
production, 47, 192; and
social reproduction, 45, 47,
115, 191; and tactics used
by people, 46, 156
Riot Act: and Bull Ring
Riots of 1839, 81; and
convictions, 68; of King
George I, 8; and Peterloo
Massacre, 71
Rioting in America (Gilje), 3,
35–6
riots: in the 1830s, 42; and
absolutization, 177–8; and
African Americans, 119–26,
122; and Alain Badiou's
work, 6–7, 40, 41–3;
anti-Asian attacks, 111;
anti-enclosure riots, 10; and
Baltimore, MD, 3, 186; and
barricades, 138; and basis
in price-setting, 191; in
Bristol, Great Britain, 52–3;
Bull Ring Riots of 1839, 81,
86–7; Chicago riots, 121–2,
183; and circulation, 16,
21, 30, 48, 122, 173, 182;
and circulation struggles,
28, 31, 46, 56, 80, 121,
124, 129, 151, 175; and
Clichy-sous-Bois, 3; and

coexistence with strikes,
116, 129; and conditions
of employment, 64; and
control of space, 138; and
Coronation Riots of King
George I, 8; and crisis,
137–8, 163; definitions of,
7, 16, 35, 37, 38, 40, 46;
and Detroit, MI, 3, 104,
105, 115, 116, 118–9; and
Detroit's Great Rebellion,
104–5, 116; disorder of,
30, 42, 83, 104, 116, 166,
184; and distinction from
the strike, 27, 123; double
riots, 179–80, 181; and
the economy, 29, 126, 179;
enclosure riots, 59; export
riots, 10, 30, 52–3, 55–7,
138, 167; and Ferguson,
MO, 3, 8, 173–4, 182–3;
and food prices, 10, 40,
50–2, 53, 177; food riots,
10, 13, 14, 28, 49, 50–2, 59,
69, 70, 82; and foreword to
*The American Revolution:
Pages From a Negro
Worker's Notebook*, 103–4;
in France, 3, 111, 154, 179;
and freeway takeovers,
8, 30, 182; and Geoffrey
Chaucer, 9; golden age of,
8, 49, 57, 60, 63, 77; and
the Gordon Riots, 53; in
Great Britain, 52–3, 111,
150, 154; Great Rebellion
in 1967, 110, 113, 116,
124; and illegality, 27, 38,
52; and India, 7; Kett's
Rebellion in 1549, 59; in
King's Lynn, Great Britain,
52–3, 54, 138; and labor
struggles, 106; and lack of a

program, 150; and lessons
from the strike tradition,
115–16; locations of, 3,
30, 36, 154; and looting,
29, 47, 82, 123, 124–5,
154, 182, 185; and Los
Angeles, CA, 3, 10–11, 154;
and machine-breaking,
65, 67–9; and *the many*,
72–3; and marketplaces,
11, 44, 55, 82, 124, 167;
and market regulation,
51–2; as matching the
mercantilist era, 57; and
meaning of the word, 8, 9;
and moral economy, 50–1;
and national riots, 55–7,
104, 105; Newark, NJ
riots, 3, 110, 123–4, 183; in
North American colonies of
England, 56; and Oakland,
CA, 3, 138, 154, 178, 179,
181; and opposition to
strikes, 4, 81–2, 83, 89;
participants in, 6–7, 16, 41,
55, 84, 166; and Peterloo
Massacre, 70–1, 81; and
police, 2, 47–8, 81, 119–20,
177; from police killings,
182–3; and political-
economic conditions,
105, 177; and political
economy, 8, 11, 13–14,
83; as a political modality,
119–20, 178–9; political
nature of, 43, 44, 47;
political reproduction of,
39; political significance of,
35; and ports, 11, 30, 52–4,
56; and poverty, 10, 163;
and price-setting, 14–16,
28, 29, 44, 46, 56, 123–5,
129, 189; and problem

of reproduction, 69–70,
172–3; and production, 46,
138–9, 172; and property,
11, 38, 81, 124, 179, 185;
and race, 27, 111–12, 122,
124, 154, 168–9; race riots,
28, 104, 111–12, 154,
168; and racialization, 11,
105, 111–12, 163–4; and
relation to crisis, 1–3, 9–10,
129; and relation to strike,
12–13, 17, 19, 68–9, 77–8,
80, 93; and reproduction,
138, 192; return of, 7, 8,
9, 10, 11, 21, 39, 72, 80;
revolutionary potential of,
4, 116, 165; and riot prime,
11, 16, 19, 21, 27–9, 46,
70, 73, 110–11, 123–4;
and riot prime's conditions,
154–5, 160, 165, 167,
170–4, 176–7; and riot
prime's locations, 187; and
riot prime's politics, 181–2,
184–6; Roubaix riots,
63–4; and seizure of food,
51–2, 82; and shift from to
strikes, 61–2, 68–70; social
content of, 84–5, 121, 150;
and social hierarchies, 9,
157–9; and spectacular
riots, 81, 84; and speech, 8;
and spontaneity, 92, 109,
166; spread of, 153–4;
and square, 11, 72, 138,
173, 176, 177, 183, 187;
against state, 11, 29, 177;
and street, 11, 138, 173,
182, 183, 187; and surplus
population, 168, 182; and
the surplus rebellion, 28;
Swing riots, 65, 67; as a
tactic of collective action,

definitions of, 7, 16, 38, 46, 61–2, 78; as dependent on capital's vitality, 85; and Detroit UAW strike, 146–7; and downing of tools, 16, 37, 144; era of, 8, 84; and factory floor, 11, 16, 173; and fight for improved wages, 61–2, 68, 87, 189; and financial resources of the proletariat, 94–5; and first strike in England, 9; Flint Glassmakers' Strike, 81–2; and French term *grève*, 62–3; and general strike of the Bakuninists, 93–4; general strikes, 72, 87, 91, 93–8, 179, 181; and horizons of socialism and communism, 89–90; and importance of 1830, 79; and labor conditions, 16, 64, 87; and legal frameworks, 27; and machine-breaking, 79; and *the many*, 73, 86; mass strikes, 91, 97–101; militant black strike, 115; narrow strikes, 12–13, 78, 91, 96; and opposition to riots, 4, 81–3, 86, 89; and political-economic conditions, 105, 121; and ports, 63; and practical circumstances, 43, 146; and prices for labor power, 15, 16, 78, 84, 139; and problem of reproduction, 69–70; and production, 16, 21, 78, 85–6, 121; proletarian and political strikes, 96; and race, 111; railroad strike of 1877, 36; and refusal to work, 87; and relation

to riot, 80–1, 87–8, 93, 115–16; and riots, 10, 11, 19, 21, 61, 63, 77–8, 110; of Russian Revolution, 99; and shift from riots to strikes, 68–70; social content of, 84–5, 121; and spontaneity, 87, 91–3, 97; as a tactic of collective action, 2, 16, 35, 38–9, 77, 80, 89, 106, 119; and transition from strike period to riot prime period, 17; in the U.K., 109; and unemployment, 107; in the U.S., 109, 118, 119; and violence, 12–13, 36–9; and workers as workers, 16, 78
Sunkara, Bhaskar, 145–6
surplus: and blackness, 120, 122, 169; of capital, 2, 162; and crisis, 162–3, 170; and growth of indebted sector, 157; and "movement of the squares" based in surplus population, 176; and politics of surplus populations, 181–2, 191; and populations in the U.S. and Europe, 183, 191; and the public, 170; and racial state violence, 164, 169; and riot prime, 170; and social surplus, 95; and surplus population, 1–2, 117, 118, 123, 154–9, 160, 164–5, 179; and the surplus rebellion, 129, 165; types of, 1–2, 162; and unemployed people, 156, 162–3, 167
Swing, Captain, 65, 66, 68

Taylorism, 134, 142
The American Revolution:

VersoBooks.com

facebook.com/
versobks

@versobooks

versobooks.
tumblr.com

@versobooks